MW01232097

ISBN: 9781313127998

Published by:
HardPress Publishing
8345 NW 66TH ST #2561
MIAMI FL 33166-2626

Email: info@hardpress.net
Web: http://www.hardpress.net

COMMON LAW MARRIAGE

AND ITS DEVELOPMENT
IN THE UNITED STATES

By

OTTO E. KOEGEL, D.C.L.

Associate Counsel, United States Veterans' Bureau, Professor of Domestic
Relations, National University Law School, Member of the Central
Committee on Hereditary Defectives in the United States of
the Second International Congress of Eugenics, Member of the Committee on Marriage Laws of
the American Association for Organizing
Family Social Work, etc.

JOHN BYRNE & COMPANY
LAW PUBLISHERS AND BOOKSELLERS
WASHINGTON, 1922

To

Honorable Charles F. Cramer, Esquire,
General Counsel U. S. Veterans' Bu-
reau and Special Assistant to the Attor-
ney General of the United States,
"A man among men,"
this work is affectionately dedicated

B 14094

TABLE OF CONTENTS

			PAGE
Introductory		....	7
Chapter	I.	Marriage Prior to The Council of Trent (1563)	11
Chapter	II.	The Council of Trent	22
Chapter	III.	The English Marriage Act of 1753	27
Chapter	IV.	The Great Controversy in England in the Nineteenth Century	37
Chapter	V.	Marriage in the American Colonies	54
Chapter	VI.	Early American decisions for and Against Common Law Marriage	76
Chapter	VII.	Chancellor Kent's Dicta, and the Development of Common Law Marriage in the United States	79
Chapter	VIII.	The Present State of the Law on the Subject	105
Chapter	IX.	Tabular Analysis and Conclusion	161
Index		....	177

INTRODUCTORY

The development of marriage as a social institution is a subject which raises some of the most perplexing problems of the whole wide field of anthropology and sociology. Whether "the first blessing God gave to man was society, and that society was a marriage and that marriage was confederate by God Himself and hallowed by a blessing,"[1] or whether "marriage and agnatic relationship belong to comparatively recent times";[2] are questions with which the law is not greatly concerned.

Again, the strictly legal aspects of marriage cover a wide area in the field of jurisprudence. Our present concern, however, is only with the legal effect of informal or irregular marriages by the common law of England and the development of that law in the United States.

Common law marriage may be defined as a marriage which does not depend for its validity upon any religious or civil ceremony but is created by the consent of the parties as any other contract. The term "common law marriage," however, is not strictly an accurate one. Some writers on the subject prefer not to call it by that name, and some of those that do, make apologies for it.

---

[1]Bishop Jeremy Taylor's Works, Ed. 1848, p. 207 (Sermon on the Marriage Ring). "Marriage was not originated by human law. When God created Eve, she was a wife of Adam; they then and there occupied the status of husband to wife and wife to husband." Grigsby v. Rieb, 105 Tex. 597 (1913) "Marriage was first instituted by God Himself in paradise between Adam and Eve," says a writer on Canon Law in 1734. (Ayliffe, Parergon Juris Canonici Anglicani, p. 359.)

[2]McLennan, Primitive Marriage, Reprinted in Studies in Ancient History, p. 87 (Macmillan Co. 1886).

At the same time the term is used by practically all at the bar, and there is no escape from it. In this discussion the term "common law marriage" will be used in two senses: One, an informal marriage recognized by the common law of England; Two, an informal marriage recognized by the law of a particular State.

There is no exhaustive treatise on the subject of common law marriage in the United States. Indeed, there is nothing on the subject except such brief discussions as are contained in works on Matrimonial Institutions, Domestic Relations, Marriage and Divorce, and a few rather copious notes in the reports.[3] Because of the lack of any adequate treatment of the subject, the Bureau of War Risk Insurance was recently obliged to compile a digest of the laws and decisions of the several states on common law marriage for use in connection with hundreds of claims founded on alleged common law marriages.[4] That compilation is extremely brief and was never intended as a treatise on common law marriage. The bibliography of the subject chiefly consists of some thirty-five articles in legal periodicals (only a very few of which exceed one page in length), the brief statements in works on Marriage and Domestic Relations, and the decisions of the courts.

This work is not intended to be a complete treatise on the subject. Its purpose is to show the development of common law marriages in the United States and the present state of the law on the subject in this country. Among the facts shown in this work are the following:

[3]Treas. Dept. Document 2834.
[4]See Bibliography.

1. That common law marriages have not been valid in England since 1753.

2. That such marriages were valid prior to that time, notwithstanding a decision of the House of Lords in 1843 that they were never valid in England.

3. That such marriages were invalid at common law for possessory purposes, that is, the children could not inherit, the wife took no dower, et cetera.

4. That such marriages were invalid in some of the American colonies, and certainly contrary to legislation and the policy of all the colonies.

5. That the earliest decisions in the United States are against the validity of such marriages, but these decisions are not referred to in the decisions establishing the rule in this country.

6. That such marriages owe much of their validity to dicta of Chancellor Kent in 1809.

7. That the Kent doctrine was not generally accepted until more than half a century later, the Supreme Court of the United States being evenly divided on the question in 1843.

8. That the early decisions in this country, both those establishing the rule and those denying it, are extremely poorly considered cases, citing no authority and of only a page or two in length, whereas, the English cases show that no one subject in their jurisprudence was ever more carefully considered, one case alone covering nearly four hundred pages.

9. That some states, apparently upholding the validity of common law marriage, have in effect discarded the rule *consensus non concubitas facit matrimonium,* and adopted

one, *concubitas facit matrimonium*. In other words, some states require cohabitation in addition to words of consent and thus we have one law providing that persons must cohabit before they become husband and wife (in itself anomalous) and another law providing that persons who do this without marrying are guilty of a crime.

10. That, strictly speaking, the common law doctrine is in most states recognized in name only; certainly in all of the states where the question has arisen marriage *per verba de futuro* has been discarded and the question of the validity of marriage *per verba de præsenti* without cohabitation has not frequently arisen.

11. That the American decisions show that the courts of this country have not carefully investigated the subject.

12. That such marriages are opposed by the American Bar Association, The Commission on Uniform State Laws, all modern authorities on Sociology, Marriage and kindred subjects and should be abolished.

CHAPTER I

MARRIAGE PRIOR TO THE COUNCIL OF TRENT 1563

Prior to the Council of Trent (1543-1563) and as far back as we have any knowledge of the Roman law[1] a celebration *in facie ecclesiæ* was not necessary to a valid marriage in those countries where the western church prevailed. And the Council of Trent itself acknowledges this in these words: "Whereas, therefore, matrimony in the evangelical law excels the ancient marriage in grace, through Christ * * * *." It must not be understood, however, that prior to the Council of Trent marriages were for the most part nonceremonial. Following the teachings of St. Paul, the Christian church from an early date numbered marriage among the sacraments. Tertullian, writing in the second century, says marriage not performed in the church (*occultæ conjunctiones*) is considered almost as bad as fornication. This fact however is frequently overlooked.[2] The following from Reeve on Domestic Relations in regard to the matter is typical of many such statements contained in our reports.

> "There is nothing in the nature of a marriage contract that is more sacred than that of other contracts that require the intervention of a person in holy orders, or that it should be solemnized in a church. Every idea of this kind, entertained by any

---

[1]By the Twelve Tables a valid marriage did not depend on any ceremony.
[2]Eversly, Domestic Relations, p. 13 (2d Ed. London, 1896); Ency. Britt. Article Marriage. Pollock and Maitland say that during Bracton's time all decent persons go to church to be married. History of English Law Bk. II, 375.

person, has arisen wholly from the usurpation of the church of Rome on the rights of the civilian. She claimed the absolute control of marriages, on the ground that marriage was a sacrament, and belonged wholly to the management of the clergy. *The solemnization of marriage by a clergyman was a thing never heard of among primitive Christians until Pope Innocent III ordered it otherwise.*"[3]

Pollock and Maitland have shown that marriage in church was a thing not only heard of but practiced even in England long before the proclamation of Innocent. III. On this point they say:

"At the Lateran Council of 1215 Innocent III extended over the whole of Western Christendom the custom that had *hitherto* obtained in some countries of 'publishing the banns of marriage.' * * * From that time forward a marriage with banns had certain legal advantages over a marriage without banns. * * * This seems the origin of the belief that Innocent III 'was the first who ordained the celebration of marriage in the church.' This belief is stated by Blackstone, Comment. I, 439, and was in his time traditional among English lawyers. Apparently, it can be traced to Dr. Goldingham, a civilian who was consulted in the case of Bunting v. Lepingwell (Moore's Reports 169).[4]

Justice Willes says that irregular and clandestine marriages were at the time of the Council of Trent looked upon as odious.[5] But, however, down to the time of the Council of Trent the canons on marriage were merely directory, without any nullifying clause, and the marriage although irregular and clandestine, was valid if the con-

---

[3]Reeve Dom. Rel. 196. The words italicized, it seems, were first quoted by J. Woodbury in 1820 (1 N. H. 278). See also Dumaresly v. Fishly, 10 Ky. 370 for same statement.

[4]Pollock & Maitland History English Law Book I, p. 370, note 371.

[5]Beamish v. Beamish, 9 H. of L. cases, p. 309.

tract was proved to have been entered into *per verba de præsenti.*[6]

Whether the rule that prevailed on the continent prior to the Council of Trent also prevailed in England, once caused much debate but it is now pretty well settled that the same was true in England. The erroneous decision of the House of Lords in Regina v. Millis in regard to the matter will be discussed later.

In any discussion of marriage at common law we must remember that in England the jurisdiction over marriage was divided between the spiritual and temporal tribunals, administering the canon and common law, respectively. This fact must never be lost sight of in a discussion of marriage at common law. Writing on the subject, one learned writer says:

> "But now that we come to consider the course which the English law of marriage has taken, let us note that this law has flowed in two distinct channels down till our time. So much of it as pertained to the marriage relation itself, that is to say, to the capacity for contracting marriage (including prohibited degrees), to the mode of contracting it, and to its dissolution, complete or partial, belonged to the canon or ecclesiastical law and was administered by the spiritual courts. So much of it as affected the property rights of the two parties (and especially rights to land) belonged to the common law and was administered in the temporal courts. This division to which there is nothing parallel in the classical Roman law, was of course due to the fact that mediæval Christianity, regarding marriage as a sacrament, placed it under the control of the church and her tribunals in those aspects which were deemed to affect the spiritual well-being of the parties to it. Nevertheless the line of demarcation

---

[6]Lord Campbell, ibid. p. 337.

between the two sides was not always, and indeed
could hardly be, sharply or consistently drawn.
The ecclesiastical courts had a certain jurisdiction
as regards property. The civil courts were obliged,
for the purposes of determining the right of a
woman to dower and the right of intestate succes-
sion, to decide whether or no a proper and valid
marriage had been contracted. The regular course
apparently was to send the matter to the bishop's
court and act upon the judgment which it pronounced. But this was not always done. They
often had to settle the question for themselves, ap-
plying no doubt, as a rule the principles which the
bishop's court would have followed, and (as has
been explained by the latest and best of our English
legal historians, Pollock and Maitland) they often
evaded the question whether there had been a ca-
nonically valid marriage by finding that, as a matter of fact, the parties had been generally taken to
have been duly wedded, and by proceeding to give
effect to the finding.''[7]

In England and on the Continent prior to the twelfth
century it seems that carnal copulation was necessary to
the validity of an informal marriage. Gratian saw no
marriage, no indissoluble bond, no *matrimonium perfec-
tum* where there had been no *carnalis copula*. But with
the advent of the canon law the old rule was superseded
and two new ones took its place.

As early as the seventh century the Church was playing

---

[7]Bryce, Studies in Hist. and Juris. Ch. XVI. On this subject Mr. Reeves
says in his History of English Law: ''Of all articles of judicial cogni-
zance which the ecclesiastical court claimed exclusively to entertain, that of
matrimony seems to have been least controverted by the temporal judges.
When marriage was admitted by the religion of the country to be a Christian sacrament, the jurisdiction of spiritual judges could not well be disputed. We accordingly find no parliamentary interposition on this head,
but the ecclesiastical court was left to decide in matrimonial causes upon
the pure principles of canonical jurisprudence.'' (3d Ed. Vol. IV, 52.)

a prominent part concerning marriage. Beginning with the Conquest in England marriage appertained to the spiritual forum. Nothing illustrates this more clearly than the famous suit of Richard de Anesty.[8] Beginning with Glanvill the marriage law of England was the canon law. The doctrine that prevailed for a while required sexual intercourse to a valid marriage. This was the theory of the classic canon law, formulated by Gratian. But before the close of the twelfth century theological subtlety had conceived and gained the acceptance of a distinction in the forms of contract which was fatal to the security of the marriage bond. The famous classification of contracts as *per verba de præsenti* and *per verba de futuro cum copula* is due mainly to Peter Lombard, a professor in the University of Paris and later an ordained bishop. His doctrine, says Howard, represents the triumph of Gallic theology over the doctrine of Gratian, as maintained by the Italian jurists, and Pollock and Maitland say it is a victory of Parisian theology over Bolognese jurisprudence. Prof. Esmein says this distinction was not invented by Peter Lombard although Lombard is responsible for the importance which was given it.[8] On this subject Pollock and Maitland say:

---

[8] An excellent account of this suit will be found in Select Essays in Anglo-American Legal History.

[9] ''Le mérite d'avoir inventé cette distinction ne paraît pas d'ailleurs revenir à Pierre Lombard. On a montré récemment qu'elle se trouvait déjà dans Hugues de Saint-Victor; elle était nettement contenue dans le droit romain classique, et le pape Innocent III' affirme dans une décrétale de la première moitié du xii siècle. Mais c'est bien Lombard qui l'a mise en pleine lumière, et qui en a tiré toutes les conséquences importantes.'' Le Mariage En Droit Canonique I, 122, citing Sehling, die Unterscheidung der Verlobnisse im kanonischen Recht, 1887, p. 60.

2

"According to the doctrine that prevailed for a while, there was no marriage until man and woman had become one flesh. In strictness of law all that was essential was this physical union accompanied by the intent to be thenceforth husband and wife. All that preceded this could be no more than an espousal (*desponsatio*) and the relationship between the spouses was one which was dissoluble; in particular it was dissolved if either of them contracted a perfect marriage with a third person. However, in the course of the twelfth century, when the classical canon law was taking shape, a new distinction came to the front. Espousals were of two kinds: *sponsalia per verba de futuro*, which take place if man and woman promise each other that they will hereafter become husband and wife; *sponsalia per verba præsenti*, which take place if they declare that they take each other as husband and wife now, at this very moment. It is thenceforth the established doctrine that a transaction of the latter kind (*sponsalia per verba de præsenti*) creates a bond which is hardly to be dissolved; in particular, it is not dissolved though one of the spouses goes through the ceremony of marriage and is physically united with another person. * * * As to *sponsalia per verba de futuro*, the doctrine of the canonists was that sexual intercourse if preceded by such espousals was a marriage; a presumption of law explained the *carnalis copula* by the foregoing promise to marry. * * * "[10]

Professor Lorenzen, a learned writer, says in regard to this subject:

"The canon law accepted as its fundamental doctrine the principle that *consensus facit nuptias*. Gratian insisted that there was no marriage unless the agreement to take each other as husband and wife was followed by cohabitation, but this requirement did not prevail. Peter Lombard, professor at the University of Paris, and later ordained bishop,

---

[10] Book II, p. 368.

suggested a distinction in this regard between *sponsalia de præsenti* and *sponsalia per verba de futuro,* requiring cohabitation only for the latter. Through the influence of Alexander III the church accepted this distinction toward the end of the twelfth and at the beginning of the thirteenth centuries.'"[11]

Pollock and Maitland say that the scheme at which Lombard and the canonists thus arrived was certainly no masterpiece of human wisdom for of all people in the world lovers are least likely to distinguish precisely between the present and the future tenses. In the Middle Ages marriages or what looked like marriages were very insecure. The validity of the marriage depended on whether the parties had said "I will" or "I do." The difference was not essential but purely verbal. A powerful protest was rendered by the legist Vacarius but he could not prevail. Luther's protest is interesting:

> "They have played a regular fool's game with their *verbis de præsenti vel futuro.* With it they have torn apart many marriages which were valid according to their own law, and those which were not valid they have bound up. Indeed I should not myself know how a churl would or could bethroth himself *de futuro* in the German tongue; for the one bethroths himself means *per verba de præsenti,* and surely a clown knows nothing of such nimble grammar as the difference between *accipio* and *accipiam;* therefore he proceeds according to our way of speech and says: 'I will have thee,' 'I will take thee,' 'thou shalt be mine.' Thereupon 'yes' is said at once without more ado." (Cited by Howard I, p. 341.)

---

[11]32 Harv. Law Review 474, citing Poll. & Mait., 1 Esmein Le Mariage En Droit Canonique, 109; 1 Howard, History of Matrimonial Institutions, 336.

The decisions themselves on these questions are often contradictory. Friedberg has shown that the Liber officialis of St. Andrews, Scotland contains the record of a divorce granted from a second union because a man had already contracted a previous marriage in these words: "I promith tò you Begis Abirnethy that I sall mary yow, and that I sall neuere haiff ane uther wiff and thereto I giff yow my fayth." Howard says it is a striking illustration of the entanglements resulting from the canonical theory that this contract is styled in the record "both *sponsalia de futuro* and *præsenti*." (Friedberg, Eheschliessung, 58; cited by Howard I, p. 344.)

The doctrine of the canonists continued to be the law of England until 1753 when Lord Hardwicke's Act made a ceremony in the Established Church essential to the validity of a marriage. Curiously enough, however, in 1843 the House of Lord, in a 400 page opinion which has now been held to be historically unsound by all competent scholars, held that by the common law a valid marriage could not be entered into except *in facie ecclesiæ*.

Although from the earliest times an English marriage could be established without showing that it had been celebrated *in facie ecclesiæ*, however, after the canon law had displaced the secular law regarding marriage, either of the parties to an informal marriage by mere words in the present, could compel the other, by a suit in the ecclesiastical court to solemnize it in due form.[12] Serious disabilities also attached to a marriage of this kind. The disabilities were: the woman could not claim dower because she had not been "endowed at the church door";

---

[12]Holland, Juris. 10th Ed. 286; Blackstone Bk. 1 ch. 15, p. 439.

the issue of the marriage was incapable of inheriting English soil; and after the Lateran Council of 1215 which provided for the publishing of banns of marriage, persons married informally were not admitted into the church.[13]

It has often been asserted, and on high authority, that the children of these informal marriages were illegitimate.[14] This was one of the strongest points urged by the Lord Chancellor in his opinion in Regina v. Millis. And as Lord Campbell in a dissenting opinion in the same case said that the legitimacy of the children is the test by which a valid marriage is to be determined, the question was of the utmost importance in that case. But as we will see later, the children of these marriages were not bastards.

Although, as we have seen, certain serious disabilities attached to a marriage not celebrated *in facie ecclesiæ*, still the formless, the unblessed marriage is a marriage. They will be compelled by spiritual censures to celebrate their marriage before the face of the church; but they were married already when they exchanged a consent *per*

---

[13]In Fitzherberts Natura Brevium it is said that a woman married in a chamber shall not have dower by the common law. Eversly Domestic Relations, 2d Ed. p. 15. ''Though the presence of a priest was necessary, the entire ceremony was not for a long time celebrated in the body of a church, but a portion was gone through at the porch (*ostium ecclesiæ*) in the presence of the neighbors and the priest. The old kind of dower *ad ostium ecclesiæ* originated in this ceremony. The bridegroom was wont to point to his lands, doubtless often visible from the porch, and called—after 'affiance and troth plighted between bride and himself'—those present to witness that he dowered her of a third of them.'' Ibid. A thorough discussion of the diabilities incident to informal marriages under the early English law, such as the inability of the children, although legitimate, to inherit, and the inability of the widow to claim dower, will be found in Pollock and Maitland's History of English Law, Bk. 11, 374 *et seq.*

[14]101 L. T. 575; Reg. v. Millis P. 848, p. 851, p. 858. Everely Domestic Relations, 2d Edition (London 1896) p. 16.

verba de præsenti, or became one flesh after exchanging a
consent *per verba de futuro.*[15]   And in Richard de Anesty's case, decided by the Pope in 1143, a marriage solemnly celebrated in church, a marriage of which a child
had been born, was set aside as null in favor of an earlier
marriage constituted by a mere exchange of consenting
words.[16]   But what seems to be decisive of the point is the
following decretal of Pope Alexander III, addressed to
the Bishop of Norwich, in the reign of Henry II:[17]

> ''We understand from your letter that a certain
> man and woman at the command of their lord mu-
> tually received each other, no priest being present,
> and no such ceremony being performed as the Eng-
> lish church is wont to employ, and then that before
> any physical union, another man solemnly married
> the said woman and knew her. We answer that if
> the first man and the woman knew each other by
> mutual consent directed to time present, saying the
> one to the other, 'I receive you as mine (*meum*),'
> and 'I receive you as mine (*meam*),' then, albeit
> there was no such ceremony as aforesaid, and albeit
> there was no carnal knowledge, the woman ought to
> be restored to the first man, for after such a consent
> she could not and ought not to marry another. If
> however there was no such consent by such words
> as aforesaid, and no sexual union preceded by a
> consent *de futuro,* then the woman must be left to

[15]Poll. & Mait. History Eng. Law Bk. II, p. 373.

[16]Ibid. 367; See Essay 33 Vol. II, Select Essays Anglo-American Legal
History.

[17]Poll. & Mait. Hisory English Law Bk. II, p. 37; also cited by Willes,
J., in Beamish v. Beamish, 9 H. of L. Cases, p. 308. This decree was not
mentioned by Judges in Regina v. Millis and Pollock and Maitland infer
that it was unknown to them. John Ayliffe, in 1734, says in his Parergon
Juris Canonici Anglicani: ''If the parties have contracted *de præsenti,*
and one of the parties should afterwards marry another person in the
face of the church, and consummate the same by carnal copulation, and
procreation of children; yet the first contract is good, and shall prevail
against the marriage'' (p. 249).

the second man who subsequently received her and knew her, and she must be absolved from the suit of the first man; and if he has given faith or sworn an oath (to marry the woman), then a pennance must be set him for the breach of faith or of his oath. But in case either of the parties shall have appealed, then, unless an appeal is excluded by the terms of the commission, you are to defer to that appeal.''

CHAPTER II

The Council of Trent

The Council of Trent marks an important date in the development of the law of marriage. This council, the nineteenth of the ecumenical councils recognized by the Roman Catholic Church takes its name from the place where it was held, a city seventy-three miles northwest of Venice, and lasted, with interruptions, from December 15, 1543, to December 4, 1563. From a doctrinal and disciplinary point of view it was the most important council in the history of the Roman Church.[1]

The object of the council was two-fold: First, to condemn the principles of Protestantism and, second, to define the doctrines of the Roman Catholic Church on all disputed points. The session that is important in this discussion is the twenty-fourth, November 11, 1563, when the *Decretum de Reformatione Matrimonii* was passed. At this session concubinage was condemned and the validity of marriage made dependent on its being performed before a priest and in the presence of two or three witnesses. This decree, however, was carried against the opinion of 56 prelates, who held that the church had no power to nullify the effect of a sacrament.

It is quite frequent that we see it stated by learned writers that the Council of Trent required a marriage to be *solemnized by a priest* in the presence of witnesses.[2]

---

[1] Schaff-Herzog, Ency. Relig. Vol. XII 2.
[2] Treas. Doc. 2834; Ency. Brittanica Article on Marriage; Ringrose, Marriage and Div. Laws of the World. p. 9; 18 Ruling Case Law 389.

Such statements are clearly erroneous. On this point
Lord Campbell, in Regina v. Millis, says:

> "The decree of the Council of Trent respecting
> the solemnization of marriage requires the pres-
> ence of the parish priest or some other priest spe-
> cially appointed by him or the Bishop; but, even
> under this decree, the priest is present merely as a
> witness; it is not necessary that he should perform
> any religious service, or in any way join in the sol-
> emnity. This view of the subject is illustrated by
> the case of Lord and Lady Herbert, 3 Phill. 58, 2
> Hagg. Cons. Rep. 263. They were married in Sic-
> ily, where the decree of the Council of Trent is re-
> ceived. They got the parish priest to attend at the
> house of the lady, and two of her servants were
> called up. In the presence of these witnesses she
> said, 'I take you for my husband,' and he said, 'I
> take you for my wife.' Nothing more passed, and
> this was held to be a valid marriage in Sicily, and
> therefore all the world over. It thus appears quite
> certain that, according to the doctrine of the Roman
> Catholic Church, no religious ceremony was or is
> necessary to the constitution of a valid marriage."[3]

And Mr. Justice Willes was of the same opinion in the
case of Beamish v. Beamish. There he said: "Upon the
construction of this decree, it has been holden that, provided the marriage takes place per verba de præsenti, in
the presence of the *parochus* and two witnesses, though
the priest take no part in the ceremony, and even dissent
from and reluct against it, the terms of the decree are
satisfied, and the marriage is valid."[4] Mr. Bishop says,
"Neither is it indispensable for the person in holy orders
to take an active part in the marriage."[5] The main ob-

[3] p. 753.
[4] 9 H. of L. Cas. 319.
[5] Marr. and Div. Sec. 392. We cannot agree with him, however, that
Beamish v. Beamish throws doubt on the point. That case merely decided
that the bridegroom, himself in holy orders, could not celebrate the marriage "in his own presence" and comply with the requirement that it be
in *facie ecclesiæ.*

ject of the provision of the Council of Trent, says Professor Lorenzen, was to give publicity to the marriage, to bring the fact of marriage to the notice of the Church.[6]

Some writers say that the council required two witnesses, while others state that it required three witnesses.[7] What the council actually did require was that the marriage be entered into in the presence of the parish priest and "two or three witnesses." Justice Willes said "this contemplates three witnesses to a marriage one of whom must be the *parochus*."[8] As the twenty-fourth session of the Council of Trent is of the greatest importance in any discussion relating to early marriage law it is well that the decrees and canons of that session relating to marriage be quoted here. They are as follows:

CANON I OF THE CANONS TOUCHING THE SACRAMENT OF MATRIMONY

Canon 1. If any one shall say, that matrimony is not truly and properly one of the seven sacraments of the evangelical law, instituted by Christ the Lord; but that it has been invented by men in the church, and that it does not confer grace; let him be anathema.

DECREE TOUCHING THE REFORMATION OF MARRIAGE

"Although it is not to be doubted, that clandestine marriages, made with the free consent of the parties contracting, are valid and true marriages, so long as the Church has not rendered them

---

[6]32 Harv. Law. Rev. 476. Pollock and Maitland say the Council of Trent very wisely made this requirement. History English Law, Bk. II. 374.

[7]Ency. Brittanica, Article on Marriage. Schaff-Herzog Ency. Religion Vol. XII, p. 3.

[8]Beamish v. Beamish, 9 H. L. Cases, 321, 322.

invalid; and consequently, that those persons are justly to be condemned, as the holy synod doth condemn them with anathema, who deny that such marriages are true and valid; as also those who falsely affirmed that marriages contracted by the children of a family, without the consent of their parents, are invalid, and that parents can make such marriages either valid or invalid; nevertheless, the holy Church of God has, for most just reasons, at all times detested and prohibited them. But, whereas the holy synod perceives that those prohibitions, by reason of men's disobedience, no longer avail; and, whereas it takes into account the grievous sins which arise from the said clandestine marriages, and especially the sins of those parties who continue in a state of damnation, when, having left their former wife, with whom they had privily contracted marriage, they publicly marry another, and live with her in perpetual adultery; an evil which the Church, which judges not of things hidden, cannot rectify, unless some more efficacious remedy be applied; therefore, treading in the footsteps of the sacred Council of Lateran, celebrated under Innocent III, it ordains that, for the future, before a marriage is contracted, it shall three times be announced publicly in the church, by the proper parish priest of the contracting parties, during the solemnization of mass, on three continuous festival days, between whom marriage is to be celebrated; after which banns being published, if there be no lawful impediment opposed, the marriage shall be proceeded with in the face of the church; where the parish priest, after having questioned the man and the woman, and having learnt their mutual consent, shall either say, "I join you together in matrimony, in the name of the Father, and of the Son, and of the Holy Ghost"; or shall use other words, according to the received rite of each province. But if there should at any time be a probable suspicion that the marriage may be maliciously hindered, if so many publications of banns have preceded it; in this case either one publication only shall be made; or at least the marriage shall be celebrated in the presence of the parish priest, and of two or three witnesses. Then, before the consummation thereof, the banns shall be published in the church; that so, if there be privily any impediments, they may the more easily be discovered: unless the ordinary shall himself judge it to be expedient, that the publications aforesaid be dispensed with, which the holy synod leaves to his prudence and judgment. *Those who shall attempt to contract marriage otherwise than in the presence of the parish priest, or of some other priest by permission of the said parish priest, or of the ordinary, and in the presence of two or three witnesses; them doth the holy synod render utterly incapable of thus contracting, and declares such contracts void and null, as by the present decree it declares such contracts void* and annuls them. Yet further, it enjoins that the parish priest, or any other priest, who shall have been present at any such contract with a less number of witnesses (than aforesaid); as also the witnesses who have been present thereat without the parish priest, or some other priest; and, also, the contracting parties themselves; shall be severely punished, at the discretion of the ordinary. *Furthermore, the same holy synod exhorts that the married couple do not live together in the same house until they have received the secerdotal benediction, which is to be received in the church;* and it ordains that the benediction shall be given by their own parish priest, and that permission to bestow the aforesaid benediction cannot be granted by any other than the parish priest himself, or the ordinary; any custom, even though immemorial, which is rather to be called a corruption, or any privilege, notwithstanding. And if any parish priest, or any other priest, whether he be regular or secular, shall dare to unite in marriage the bethrothed of another parish, or to bless them (when married), without the permission of their parish priest, he shall, even though he may contend that he is allowed to do this by a privilege, or an immemorial custom, remain by the very act suspended, until he be absolved by the ordinary of that parish priest who ought to have been present at the marriage, or from whom the benediction ought to have been received. The parish priest shall have a book, which he shall keep carefully by him, in the which he shall register the names of the parties married, and of the witnesses, and the time and place of the marriage being contracted. Finally, the holy synod exhorts those who marry, that, before they contract, or, at all events, three days before the consummation of marriage, they carefully confess their sins, and approach piously to the most holy sacrament of the Eucharist. If any provinces have herein in use any praiseworthy customs and ceremonies, besides the aforesaid, the holy synod earnestly desires that they by all means be retained. And lest these so wholesome injunctions be unknown to any, it enjoins on all ordinaries, that they, as soon as they are able, take care that this decree be published and explained to the people in every parish church of their respective dioceses; and that this be done as often as possible during the first year; and afterwards, as often as they shall begin to have its effect in each parish at the expiration of thirty days, to be reckoned from the day of its first publication made in the said parish.''⁹

It will be seen from the foregoing that the Council recognized the validity of informal marriages theretofore entered into; and although it anathematizes any one who shall say that marriage is not a sacrament and exhorts the married couple not to live together until they have received the sacerdotal benediction, declares invalid only those marriages not contracted in the presence of the parish priest and two or three witnesses.

---

⁹Canons and Decrees, Council of Trent, Buckley, London 1851.

As to the effect the Council of Trent had on the subject of marriage one learned writer says:

> This great Council, which was intended to secure the union of Christendom under the See of Rome, really contributed to intensify the separatist forces then at work: and from it onwards one can no longer speak of a general marriage law even for Western Europe. Custom and legislation took thenceforward different courses, not only as between Protestant and Roman Catholic nations, but even different Protestant nations, there being no common ecclesiastical authority which Protestant States recognized.'"[10]

No attempt was made to introduce the decrees of the Council of Trent into England. Pius IV did request Mary, queen of Scots to publish them in Scotland, but the Reformation was on and she dared not do it. But in all countries where the decrees of the Council of Trent have been accepted informal marriages (or, so-called, common law marriages) are not recognized.

---

[10] Bryce, Studies in Hist. and Juris. Ch. XVI.

CHAPTER III

THE ENGLISH MARRIAGE ACT OF 1753

The validity of marriage at common law is not of much practical importance in England today. By the Marriage Act of 1753 such marriages were rendered invalid. This may appear to be common knowledge as it is mentioned by Blackstone but the following recent statement is evidence that it is not. "In England it was long held that contracts of marriage *per verba de præsenti* were valid. * * * However, in the year 1844, what thus had been regarded as a rule of the common law, as derived from the ecclesiastical law, was overturned by the House of Lords, which being evenly divided on the question of the validity of a marriage *per verba de præsenti,* resolved it in the negative, *and later* the English Marriage Act expressly rendered void marriages which were not solemnized in accordance with its provisions."[1]

In the nineteenth century, however, several great controversies arose concerning the validity of informal marriages in Scotland and Ireland and the solution of these questions depended on the common law as it existed prior to the Act of 1753. This will be considered in the next chapter.

The Act of 1753 was made necessary, in a large measure, because of the great number of clandestine marriages and because of the loose and easy manner in which matri-

[1] Ruling Case Law, vol. 18, Sec. 390; Treas. Dept. Doc. 2834; See also Grigsby v. State, 105 Tex. 597, where it is stated that common law marriages were abolished in England in 1823.

mony could be accomplished. Chief among the abuses
was the so-called Fleet marriage of which a few words
may be said. Beginning with the reign of William III a
number of acts were passed designed to check marriages
constituted without any formality. These acts provided
for a fine against both the minister officiating and the parties to the marriage where banns was not published.
These statutes however proved ineffective. The Fleet
was the prison in which formerly all prisoners for debt
from the entire kingdom were, or could demand to be,
confined. On account of the scant accommodation for the
vast number congregated there, it became customary to
allow those who could give security for appearance when
wanted to take private lodgings anywhere within the
"rules of liberties" of the Fleet, a portion of London of
considerable area and well defined limits. Here were
confined many disreputable clergymen, perhaps deprived
of their benefices for misconduct; these were the Fleet
parsons. These parsons would marry matrimonially inclined couples cheaply, without banns or witnesses; present the parties with a "certificate" and make them believe they had been married in the most solemn manner.
Of course the marriages were legal and would have been
valid as marriages *per verba de præsenti* without the
"minister" but such marriages were even at that time in
the worst possible taste. Such a marriage had many advantages. It saved the parties a fine and a record was
kept, such as it was. The following instances illustrate
the magnitude and character of this "business."

"Yesterday," said the Old Whig of April 14, 1737,
"Parson Gaynham, near eighty years of age, very

remarkable for having coupled thirty-six thousand couples in the Liberty of the Fleet, was himself married in the same Liberty to his servant maid, who has lived with him upwards of fourteen years.''

The following illustrates the manner in which the entries in the ''register'' were made:

''September 29, 1736, John Bennett Turner of St. Clement Danes and Barbara Munden Batchelor and Spinster. He a little old man about 60 years of age and very effeminate in voice, Domi Silk Clark'' ''N. B. they had lived together four years as man and wife; they were so vile as to ask for a certificate to be antidated.''

These ''parsons'' were great advertisers. Their advertisements ran about as follows:

''J. Lilley at ye Hand and Pen, next door to the China Shop, Fleet Bridge, London, will be perform'd the solemnization of marriage by a gentleman regularly bred at one of our Universities, and lawfully ordain'd according to the institutions of the Church of England, and is ready to wait on any person in town or country.''

Some of the ''parsons'' were the worst kind of fakers. The system had grown to such an extent that even in 1755 *after* the passage of the Marriage Act, one Keith performed 1,190 bannless marriages during the year. His conviction rendered void some 1,400 marriages.[2]

The situation was so bad that a number of books were written urging the passage of a law to curb these clandestine marriages.[3]

The proximate cause of the passage of Hardwicke Act

[2] For an excellent summary see Howard History Matrimonial Institutions, Vol. I, p. 435.

[3] One of the best arguments against them is Gally, Clandestine Marriages. London, 1755.

3

of 1753 was the celebrated case of Cochrane v. Campbell, which came before the House of Lords in the same year. Save for lack of evidence of the alleged prior contract, "the wife who in true love during so long a time had been devoted to her husband, though already dead, would have been degraded to the position of a concubine, the children begotten in marriage branded as bastards, and robbed of their inheritance."[4]

26 George II c. 33.[5]

This act passed in 1753 became effective March 25, 1754. It is entitled "An Act for the better preventing clandestine marriages." The principal provisions are as follows: All banns of marriage shall be according to the words prescribed by the Rubrick prefixed to the office of matrimony in the Book of Common Prayer. The minister must sign the publication and the marriage must be solemnized in one of the churches where the banns have been published. Notice of the names, places of abode, and time of residence of the parties must be given to the minister seven days before publication of banns. The minister is not punishable by ecclesiastical censures for solemnizing marriage after banns have been published, where the parents or guardians give notice of dissent; but where such dissent shall be given, publication of banns are void. Licenses are to be granted to solemnize matrimony in the church or chapel of such parish only, where one of the parties shall have resided for four weeks before unless they dwell in an extra-parochial place, then in some Par-

---

[4]Howard, Hist. Matrimonial Institutions, Vol. I, p. 448.
[5]Vol. 7, Great Brit. Stats. at Large, p. 525 (London, 1769).

ish Church adjoining the extra-parochial place. The Archbishop of Canterbury's right to grant special licenses is
reserved, the act providing that it shall not deprive the
Archbishop of Canterbury and his proper officers of their
rights under Stat. 25 Henry VIII entitled "An Act concerning Peter Pence and Dispensations." Persons convicted of solemnizing marriage without banns or license,
or in any other place than in Church as aforesaid are to
be transported to "some of his Majesty's Plantations in
America for the space of fourteen years, according to the
laws in force for transportation of felons" and "all
marriages solemnized from and after the twenty-fifth
day of March in the year 1754, in any other place than a
Church or Public Chapel, unless by special license as
aforesaid, or that shall be solemnized without publication of banns, or License of Marriage from a person or
persons having authority the same first had and obtained,
shall be null and void to all intents and purposes whatsoever."

It is further provided that proof of the parties dwell-
ing in the parishes where marriages are solemnized is
not necessary to the validity of such marriages. Marriages solemnized by license without consent of the parents or guardians where either of the parties (not being
a widow or widower) shall be under age, are void. No
suit can be had in the ecclesiastical court to compel a
marriage *in facie ecclesiæ* by "reason of any contract
of matrimony whatsoever whether *per verba de præsenti*
or *per verba de futuro*." Church wardens are to provide books in which are to be registered all marriages
and banns, the same to be signed by the minister; and

the books are to belong to the parish and are to be kept for public use. Marriages must be solemnized in the presence of two witnesses, besides the {minister, and must be signed by the minister, parties and witnesses. The entry is to be made in the following manner:

"AB of .... Parish and CD of .... Parish were married in this Church (or chapel) by (Banns or License) with consent of (Parents or Guardians) this ....day of .... in the year ...... By me J. J. (Rector, Vicar or Curate). This marriage was solemnized between us (AB and CD) in the presence of (EF and GH)."

Persons convicted of making false entry in the said register or of forging any such entry, or of forging any such license or of destroying with an ill intent such register are to suffer death.

Marriages of the Royal family and of Quakers and Jews, and of persons in Scotland, or beyond the seas are excepted. The act is to be read in all Parish Churches and public Chapels on some Sunday in each of the months of September, October, November, December of 1753 and afterwards at the same time on four several Sundays for two years. The harsh provisions of this act brought forth a great deal of criticism, especially from those who were in opposition to the established church. While the act was designed to remedy the evils of clandestine marriages it really went to the opposite extreme.

This act gave rise to the Gretna Green marriages, so called from a town just across the border in Scotland where many English couples went to be married without license or banns. The "ceremony" was performed by the blacksmith or some other person and the parties immediately returned to England where the marriage was valid on the principle that a marriage valid where celebrated is valid everywhere.

Martin Madon in his Thelyphthora or Treatise on Female Ruin ("With many other incidental matters; Particularly including an examination of the principles and tendency of Stat. 26, Geo. II, c. 33, commonly called the Marriage Act") says: "Were we to search the whole history of the world, we should hardly find many inhabitants of it, without some marriage ceremony or other, and this, because nature itself, as now circumstanced, seems to point out a necessity for some outward recognition of so important a contract; for, as the corruption of human nature is to be found in all the naturally engendered offspring of fallen Adam, so the dire effects of it have made it necessary to guard against them by some means or other."[6] He bitterly attacks the requirement of a religious ceremony in the established Church by the Marriage Act, however, and makes an almost absurd comparison of it with the vulgar Hottentot marriage ceremony which he quotes from Kolben's Cape History, Vol. 1, p. 153.

The Act of 1753 was conceived in a spirit of bigoted intolerance toward all dissenters, save only Quakers and Jews. If it turned out that the Chapel was not duly consecrated the marriage was void. A man was enabled to marry a woman in the church and live with her twenty-

[6]Vol. 3, p. 315 (London, 1781).

five years and have issue by her and afterwards have the marriage annulled on the ground that he himself had sworn falsely as to her age, she being two months younger than twenty years. (Hewitt v. Bratcher 18-9; Johnson v. Parker, 3 Phillim. 39-1819.) In another case where a father had gone to America and was supposed to be dead a marriage was declared void after eighteen years cohabitation because the father had not given his consent. In another case nullity was declared because the testamentary guardians who consented were appointed by a will which turned out to be invalid because attested by only one witness.[7]

It became necessary to amend the Hardwicke Act and after numerous attempts the Civil Marriage Act of 1836 was passed which, with a few later modifications, is the law today.

---

[7]Howard, History Matrimonial Institutions, Vol. I, p. 464.

CHAPTER IV

THE GREAT CONTROVERSY IN THE 19TH CENTURY

The three important decisions bearing on the controversy as to the validity of informal marriages at common law are of such length as to justify a somewhat lengthy discussion of them here. The first of these cases (including exhibits) covers 249 pages in the report; the second covers 373 pages; the third covers 86 pages; the three cases total 708 pages.

Dalrymple v. Dalrymple, 2 Hagg. Const. 54-137.

This was a case of restitution of conjugal rights brought by the wife against the husband, in which the chief point in discussion was, the validity of a Scotch marriage, *per verba de præsenti,* and without religious celebration. Briefly, the facts were these: John William Henry Dalrymple was the son of a Scotch noble family and at the age of nineteen, being a cornet in His Majesty's dragoon guards, went with his regiment to Scotland in 1804. Shortly after his arrival, he became acquainted with Miss Johanna Gordon, the daughter of a wealthy Scotch gentleman. The evidence showed that the young Dalrymple had reasons for supposing that his father would disapprove of his connection with Miss Gordon and he enjoined her to the strictest secrecy, and this she observed until in 1808 when Mr. Dalrymple, after a long absence from Scotland with his regiment, returned to England and married Miss Laura Manners in the most

formal and regular manner. In support of her contention that she was the wife of Mr. Dalrymple, Miss Gordon
produced a number of papers inscribed ''Sacreed Promises and Engagements'' and the papers were proved to
be in the handwriting of herself and Mr. Dalrymple.
These papers were mutual acknowledgments of the parties that they were husband and wife. There was proof
that several nocturnal interviews had taken place between
them and on these occasions they had sexual intercourse.
The case was argued by men of great learning and
ability and depositions were received from some of the
greatest lawyers in Scotland, including Erskine. The
opinion and exhibits in the case cover 249 pages in the
report. The opinion was written by Sir William Scott
(Lord Stowell) and is considered a masterpiece of legal
literature. Referring to this case, one author says:
''Several of Lord Stowell's ecclesiastical decisions are
still leading cases. All of them display his remarkable
lucidity of expression and his extreme familiarity with
the Roman and Canon law.''[1] Another says this decision
is ''a masterpiece of judicial eloquence.''[2] Another calls
it ''the celebrated opinion for which learning and ele-
gance of diction has seldom been equalled.''[3] And Bishop
says it is ''a production of matchless beauty and learning, quite unsurpassed in forensic discussion.''[4] Such
then is the testimony as to the importance of this opinion.

The question was governed by the law of Scotland, the
country where the marriage took place. As the Marriage

---

[1]Sherman, Roman Law, Vol. I, 384.
[2]Schouler, Dom. Rel.
[3]Reeves, Dom. Rel. 251.
[4]Marriage, Div. and Sep. Bk. I, 398.

Act of 1753 was not applicable to Scotland, the validity of the marriage depended on what was the common law as to informal marriages. The court held that by the canon law rules as to marriage, in force in the Christian countries on the continent prior to the Council of Trent and in Scotland at the time of the marriage, informal marriages were valid, and, therefore, the marriage to Miss Gordon was valid and the marriage to Miss Manners was void. The court also said that such marriages were valid in England prior to the Marriage Act of 1753.

Regina v. Millis, 10 Cl. and Fin. 534-907.

In January 1829, George Millis (in the Kingdom of Ireland), a member of the established Church of England and Ireland, accompanied by Hester Graham (spinster), a Protestant dissenter, went to the house of Rev. John Johnstone, a regularly placed minister of the Presbyterian Church, and then entered into a present contract of marriage with the said Hester Graham; the minister performing a religious ceremony between them according to the usual form of the Presbyterian Church in Ireland. After the contract and ceremony the parties cohabited and lived together as husband and wife for a period of two years, Hester being after the time of the ceremony known by the name of Millis. After two years of married life, the parties separated but were never divorced. On December 24, 1836, five years after the separation, and while Hester was still living, Millis was married to one Jane Kennedy (spinster) in England according to the forms of the Established Church. In 1842 Millis was indicted for bigamy and pleaded not guilty. The question depended on the validity of the first marriage. The case was brought to the House of Lords on a writ of error. Questions were then put to the judges. Lord Chief Justice Tindall delivered the opinion of the judges which was unanimous as to the conclusion that the defendant was not guilty. The opinion of the House of Lords was also not guilty, but the Lords were divided. Lyndhurst (Lord Chancellor), Lord Cottenham, and Lord Abinger held the first contract was not a valid marriage. Lord Brougham, Lord Denam, and Lord Campbell held that it was. Because of the form in which the case before the House the rule *semper præsumitur pro negante* applied and the defendant was acquitted.

None of the decisions for acquittal is satisfactory. In a comparatively short opinion Lord Chief Justice Tindall overruled the Dalrymple case so far as it regards England. After his reference to Sir William Scott as "that very learned judge, in his deservedly celebrated judgment in that case" and stating that "the opinion of that eminent person so far as regards England was uncalled for and extrajudicial," it would seem that the opinion of the Judges would show clearly the inaccuracy of the decision in the Dalrymple case. But the opinion of the judges does not do it. In fact they state in their opinion that insufficient time had been given them for a decision.

Concerning this case Mr. Bishop in his work on Marriage, Divorce and Separation says:

> "We have here a question of almost pure ecclesiastical law, submitted to a tribunal composed of common-law and equity lawyers, who necessarily possessed little or no knowledge of the subject. So they asked advice, not from the ecclesiastical judges,

whose functions had qualified them to give it, but from the uninstructed common-law judges. The latter were competent to learn, but they were not allowed the necessary time. Lord Chief-Justice Tindal, who delivered their opinion, complained of the want of time for investigation; and the opinion throughout shows the complaint to have been well founded. Thereupon the law Lords, with this unintelligent advice before them, and not one of them being an ecclesiastical judge, or otherwise possessing any special knowledge of the subject, proceed, not by a majority opinion, but by separate opinions equally divided, to overturn what that matchless ecclesiastical judge Lord Stowell has held on the amplest investigation, and what every other ecclesiastical judge, both before and since, has deemed to be the true law.'' (Vol. I, Sec. 401.)

By far the most satisfactory opinion in the Millis case is the dissenting opinion of Lord Campbell.[5] After expressing his regret that the judges had not been allowed the time which they themselves stated they considered necessary for a thorough investigation of the authorities, Lord Campbell makes some interesting observations, some of which are the following:

''In the present case we have particularly to lament that we are informed of the reasoning only of one judge, as he states that 'it was only after considerable fluctuation and doubt in the minds of some of his brethren that they had acceded to the opinion which was formed by the majority.' I should have been much gratified and edified by being informed of the course of this fluctuation; what the doubts were which weighed in the minds of those learned

[5]His opinion has been called the *locus classicus* on the subject. Shakespeare's Law, Sir George Greenwood, p. 42. And the Supreme Court of the District of Columbia has said that Lord Campbell's opinion in this case is ''one of the ablest opinions that has ever been written.'' Thomas v. Holtzman, 7 Mackey 66.

persons, and by what train of reasoning those doubts were dispelled.''

''The condition contended for as indispensable to the validity of marriage, is the *presence* of a person *believed* by the parties to be in priest's or deacon's orders. It is not considered essential that he should pronounce a benediction, or join in any religious ceremony; and though he never was episcopally ordained either as a priest or deacon, his *presence* is sufficient if the parties *believe* that he is in priest's or deacon's orders; while a marriage *celebrated* by a clergyman who is *actually* in Presbyterian orders and who is believed by the parties to be entitled by the law of God and the law of the land to marry them effectually, is a nullity.''

Lord Campbell ventures to say that for more than one hundred and thirty years prior to this decision ''the opinion of all the greatest judges who have presided in Westminster Hall and in Doctor's Commons has been, that by the common law the presence of a priest in orders was not indispensably necessary to the celebration of a valid marriage.'' He then says: ''I do not find the subject again discussed till the publication of Blackstone's Commentaries, where, if anywhere, we may look to find the principles of our jurisprudence. If he has fallen into some minute mistakes in matter of detail, I believe upon a great question like this as to the constitution of marriage, there is no authority to be more relied upon. He began, before the Marriage Act, to read the lectures at Oxford, which became the Commentaries, but did not publish them till after, and his attention must have been particularly directed to the law of marriage. Does he say that at common law, marriage could not be contracted in England without the intervention of a priest? His words are 'Our law considers marriage in no other light than as a civil contract; the *holiness* of the matrimonial state is left entirely to the ecclesiastical law.' (1 Bl. Comm. 437.) He lays it down in the most express terms, that before the Marriage Act, in England a marriage *per verba de præsenti,* without the intervention of a priest, was *ipsum matrimonium.* Blackstone mentions the Marriage Act and then says, 'Much may be said and much has been said both for and against this innovation upon our ancient laws and constitution.' He adds 'Any contract made *per verba de præsenti,* or in words of the present tense, and, in case of cohabitation, *per verba de futuro* also, between persons able to contract was before the late Act deemed a valid marriage to many purposes.' This passage is to be found in the twenty-five editions of his work, which have now for a period approaching to a century taught the law of England to this country and to all civilized nations who have had any curiosity to inquire into our polity.''

"At last came the case of Dalrymple v. Dalrymple, which was for many years understood to have finally settled the law by judicial decision. I believe it is universally allowed that Lord Stowell was the greatest master of the civil and the canon law that ever presided in our courts, and that is the most masterly judgment he ever delivered. I have read it over and over again, and always with fresh delight. For lucid arrangement, for depth of learning, for accuracy of reasoning, for felicity of diction, it is almost unrivalled.''

Lord Campbell then proceeds to show that "ever since Dalrymple v. Dalrymple, every judge who has touched

upon the subject has unhesitatingly adhered to the law
as there laid down by Lord Stowell.'' He cites Lord
Ellenborough for the statement ''Now certainly a contract of marriage *per verba de præsenti* would have bound
the parties before the Act.'' He quotes Lord Chief Justice Wynford for this statement: ''The Dalrymple case
has placed it beyond a doubt that a marriage so celebrated
as this has been, would have been valid in this country
before the Marriage Act.'' He quotes Lord Tenderton,
''As I understand the law before the Marriage Act a
marriage might be even celebrated without a clergyman.''
He quotes the then Dean of the Arches, a learned civilian,
''Before the Marriage Act, marriages without a religious
ceremony might be valid, though irregular, the parties
and the minister might be liable to punishment, but the
vinculum matrimonii was not affected.'' Lord Campbell
then cites a number of criminal cases where persons were
convicted of bigamy in Ireland, the marriage being performed by dissenting ministers, one of which was the
case of Lathroppe Murray convicted of bigamy in 1815
on facts identical to the case of Regina v. Millis.

Lord Campbell also directs attention to the United
States. Says he: ''I cannot refrain from asking your
Lordships to consider how the subject has been viewed
by our brethren in the United States of America. They
carried the common law of England along with them,
and jurisprudence is the department of human knowledge to which, as pointed out by Burke, they have chiefly
devoted themselves, and in which they have chiefly ex-
celled.'' He then cites Kent and Story in support of
the general rule that informal marriages are valid. Hav-

ing shown that the law for nearly two centuries had recognized informal marriages as legal, Lord Campbell then urges that the rule of *stare decisis* be adhered to. On this he says: "Had I regarded the question as originally more doubtful, I should have thought it right to adhere to decisions by which the law has been considered settled for half a century. On questions of property it has often been said that it is the duty of a judge to support decisions which have been sometime acquiesced in and which have been acted upon, even if he would not have concurred in them when they were pronounced; lest titles should be taken. Does not this rule apply with infinitely greater force to questions of status, and most of all to questions respecting marriage on which the happiness of individuals and the welfare of society so essentially depend?"

Speaking of the decision in Regina v. Millis, Professor Pollock says: "In 1843 it has been held in this not highly convincing manner, that by the old common law of England the presence of a priest was necessary to the civil if not canonical validity of a marriage: an opinion which in 1861 was believed by a majority of the House of Lords and the judges who advised them, and is now believed by most competent scholars to be without any real historical foundation.'" And Pollock and Maitland say: "If the victorious cause pleased the lords, it is the vanquished cause that will please the historian of the middle ages.'" This view seems to have been taken by

---

[6]First Book of Jurisprudence, 328.

[7]History of English Law Bk. II, p. 372; See also Bryce, Studies in History and Jurisprudence, Ch. XVI.

practically all modern authorities on the subject. Yet
we read in a decision of the Supreme Court of California
in 1912 the following:

> "At common law the ceremony of marriage was
> religious, and to a valid marriage such ceremony
> was a pre-requisite." (Estate of Baldwin, 162
> Cal. 471.)

This statement for which no authority was cited also
appears in the syllabus of the decision in the case. It is
but one of the great number of instances shown in this
work of the unreliability of statements appearing in the
decisions of the courts of this country on the subject of
common law marriage.

In Hulett v. Cary (66 Minn. 327) and in many other
cases it has been said that the Millis case was never
recognized as authority in England. This, however, is
erroneous. The following from the Law Times (London)
October 24, 1896, answers the question.

> "The differences of opinion on the subject, though
> at the time they weighed on the minds of the judges
> and seemed to create uncertainty as to the law, must
> now be forgotten and the law regarded as absolutely
> settled. At least, that is the view that Lord Camp-
> bell, Lord Chancellor, took in 1860 in the case of
> Attorney General v. Dean and Canons of Windsor:
> (6 Jur. N. S. 834). In that case the Lord Chan-
> cellor said that the House of Lords had decided
> 'that by the common law of England a valid mar-
> riage could not be contracted without the presence
> of a priest canonically ordained. I by no means
> concurred in that decision, thinking that the com-
> mon law of England accorded with the canon law
> upon this subject, which prevailed over the whole
> of the Western Church till the Council of Trent,
> and that a valid marriage might be contracted by
> the solemn assent of the contracting parties, as

Lord Stowell had often laid down, and for fifty years had been considered clear law in Westminster Hall. But subsequently, when presiding as Chief Justice of the Queens Bench, I several times, with the approbation of my brother judges ruled that the question as to the validity of such marriages was settled by the decision of the House of Lords in Regina v. Millis. And if the question were again to be mooted in this House upon appeal, I conceive that this House would be bound to decide that such a marriage was always null and void, although Regina v. Millis was improperly decided, and that in England, till Lord Hardwicke's Act, the presence of a priest was as little necessary for making binding marriage contract as a binding contract of hire and service.' This effectually disposes of the statement of Mr. Justice Willes in 1856, in Reg. v. Mainwaring, (Dears. & B. C. C. 132), that he should never consider Regina v. Millis as a binding authority. *The common law, therefore, is definitely ascertained to be that the presence of a priest bearing orders conferred by episcopal authority is necessary to make a marriage perfect.*''

In 1861 the question was again mooted in the House of Lords where Regina v. Millis was followed in the case of Beamish v. Beamish. Doctor Samuel John Beamish died in 1852 leaving certain estates in Cork, Ireland. He had several sons of whom the Rev. Samuel Swayne Beamish was the first, and Benjamin S. Beamish, the second. Rev. Samuel Swayne Beamish died in 1844, eight years before the death of his father. On the death of Dr. Beamish, his grandson, Henry Albert Beamish, the eldest son of Rev. S. S. Beamish, claimed the right, as the eldest son of the Doctor's eldest son, to enter into possession of the estates. This claim was contested by his uncle, Benjamin Swayne Beamish, on the ground that

4

there had not been a valid marriage between the Rev. S. S. Beamish and Isabella Fraser.

The Rev. S. S. Beamish, in the year 1831, became attached to a young lady named Isabella Fraser (both being members of the United Church of England and Ireland) and as he did not obtain his father's consent to his marriage he persuaded her into a clandestine marriage, the religious ring ceremony being performed by Rev. Beamish, himself. Only the parties to the marriage were present in the room where the same was performed.

The Court of Queens Bench in Ireland found in favor of the validity of the marriage and this was affirmed by the Exchequer Chamber. The case was then brought up to the House of Lords. The question was put to the judges and Mr. Justice Willes in a learned opinion on behalf of himself and brethren, (which opinion Pollock and Maitland say is the best criticism of Regina v. Millis) decided against the validity of the marriage, solely on the authority of Regina v. Millis. This same judge had said some five years previously in another case that he should never consider the Millis case as a binding authority.[8] The case was then considered by the Lords who finally decided that the marriage was invalid.

Lord Campbell also wrote an opinion in this case and although he was more convinced than ever that Regina v. Millis was incorrectly decided, he felt obliged to follow that decision. Lord Wensleydale who was one of the

---

[8]Reg. v. Mainwaring (Dears. & B. C. C. 132). The learned annotator to Grigsby v. Rieb, L. R. A. 1915 E, also states, on the authority of the Beamish Case, that so far as England is concerned the decision in Regina v. Millis stands as law. See also Laws of England by the Earl of Halsbury (1911), Vol. 16, p. 279, to the same effect, citing Regina v. Millis.

judges who concurred in the unanimous advice given to the Lords in the Millis case expressed doubts about the matter in the Beamish case. He said:

> "If the case of the Queen v. Millis, of which we have heard so much, was now before us, to be reviewed on appeal, I am by no means sure that I should not agree in the opinion of my noble and learned friend on the woolsack. I was one of the judges who concurred in the unanimous advice given to the House in that case, but I did so with considerable difficulty. I was anxious for farther time for consideration, but the argument having taken place on the eve of the long vacation, the case could not be disposed of during that session if farther time had been allowed. The consideration I could give the case was, that, though I had very great doubt, I could not satisfy myself to give an opinion contrary to that of my colleagues, and therefore I yielded to it. I am not sure that I was the only one of the judges in the same condition.
>
> "The question is not, however, now open for consideration. It has been finally and irrevocably settled by this House, though their Lordships who gave their opinions were equally divided." (He refers to Regina v. Millis.)

The case of Beamish v. Beamish is one of the leading cases for the principle that the House of Lords is bound by its own decisions, a principle which has never been recognized by the courts of this country.[9] Sir Frederick Pollock severely criticizes this principle and a brief but intelligent discussion of the principle as applied in the cases of Regina v. Millis and Beamish v. Beamish is contained in his First Book of Jurisprudence.[10]

There is now no doubt that the decisions in these two

---

[9]The Legal Tender Cases, 12 Wallace 457 (1870).

[10]2d Edition (1904), p. 326 *et seq.*

cases were incorrect. The two cases which weighed most heavily on the minds of the judges in the Millis case have been found to have been erroneously reported. These cases are Del Heith's Case and Foxcroft's Case. The Lord Chancellor, in Regina v. Millis, referring to these cases said:

"I pass from the question of dower to that of legitimacy. One of the earliest cases upon the subject is that of Del Heith (Harl. MSS. 2117, Rogers' Ecc. Law. 584), so frequently mentioned, which was decided in the 24 Edw. I. It was as follows: John Del Heith, brother of Peter Del Heith, held lands in Bishopsthorpe near Norwich, and kept a woman named Katherine, in concubinage, by whom he had two children, Edmund and Beatrice. Being taken ill, he was advised by the vicar of Plumstead, for the good of his soul, to marry her. As he was unable to go to church, the ceremony was performed in his own house by the vicar, when the said John Del Heith pronounced the usual words, and placed a ring upon her finger; but no mass was celebrated. From that time the parties lived together as man and wife, and had another son called William. On the death of John Del Heith, his brother Peter entered upon his lands as his next heir; but a writ of ejectment was brought by the said William as son and heir of the deceased. It was asked on the trial whether any espousals were celebrated between his parents in the face of the church, after his father recovered from his illness. And because it was not proved that John Del Heith was ever married to Katherine in the face of the church, the jury found that the plaintiff had no right to the lands; thus proving that he was illegitimate.

"Foxcroft's Case, 1 Roll. Abr. 359, which occurred in the same reign, viz., in the 10 Edw. I, is to the same effect. The marriage not having been solemnized in *facie ecclesiae,* the issue was held to be illegitimate."

CASES OF DEL HEITH AND FOXCROFT   51

Relying on these same cases, Lord Chelmsford said in Beamish v. Beamish.

> "The cases of Del Heith and Foxcroft, both decided in the reign of Edw. I, established this position to its full extent. I do not find that these decisions were ever questioned until the case of The Queen v. Millis, when some of the noble and learned Lords expressed their opinion that they had been decided contrary to law. But I agree with my noble and learned friend, Lord Lyndhurst, in thinking that there is no sufficient ground for impugning their authority."

A very learned English writer in 1896 also says:

> "In Foxcroft's Case a man, shortly before his death, and while infirm and in his bed, was privately married to a women then *en ciente* by him. The marriage was performed by the bishop, but without the celebration of the mass. It was held to be void, and the issue adjudged a bastard.'"[11]

And, in 1911 we find the Supreme Court of Illinois saying:

> "The ecclesiastical courts of England had exclusive jurisdiction to determine the question of the legality of a marriage, and as a result of the holdings of that court the wife of such a marriage was not entitled to dower, and the children of the marriage were illegitimate." (Lavery v. Hutchinson, 249 Ill. 86.)[12]

---

[11]Eversly, Domestic Relations, p. 15. In a fifty-five page note on the Law Relative to the Solemnization of Matrimony, Mr. Jacob, Editor second edition of Roper on Husband and Wife, states that the issue in Foxcroft's case was adjudged a bastard. He also cites a number of cases to show that informal marriages were invalid for possessory purposes and concludes that such marriages were therefore illegal. Mr. Parsons in his work on Contracts (1853) thinks Jacob's conclusions are correct (8th Ed. Bk. III, p. 79w). Shelford in his work on Marriage and Divorce also thinks Mr. Jacob is correct. (London, 1841, p. 37.)

[12]The books are full of such statements. The statement is also made in the leading case of Davis v. Stouffer (132 Mo. App. 570, 1908).

Pollock and Maitland (1898) have found these cases in the original records, one of which was known to the Lords only through a note in a Harlein MS. of no authority. Del Heith's Case does not decide that the issue of an irregular marriage is illegitimate. It only decides that such a marriage *is no marriage for purely possessory purposes*. Dower and the right of inheritance are merely incidents of the marriage relation. Marriage may well exist without either of them. As Lord Stowell said in Lindo v. Belisario (1 Consìst. 230) "marriage may be good independent of any considerations of property, and the *vinculum fidei* may well subsist without them."[13]

Foxcroft's (correct Foxcote's) Case is not decisive since in that case it was sought to prove a marriage in church. Not only have Pollock and Maitland proved that these two cases were misunderstood but they have shown conclusively that the children of these informal marriages were legitimate.[14] On this point they say:

> "As to the particular point that has been disputed, we have Bracton's word that a marriage which was not contracted *in facie ecclesiæ*, though it cannot give the wife a claim to dower, may well be a good enough marriage so far as regards the legitimacy of the children. A case which had occurred shortly before he wrote his treatise shows us that he had good warrant for his assertion.
> "In or about 1254 died one William de Cardunville, a tenant in chief of the crown. In the usual course an *inquisitio post mortem* was held for the

---

[13]Although by the common law there is no dower where there is no marriage as is expressed by the maxim *ubi nullium matrimonium, ibi nulla dost est*, yet the converse was not also true, that is there is no marriage where there is no dower. This distinction was not observed by the judges in the Millis case.

[14]History of Eng. Law, Bk. II, 384.

purpose of finding his heir. The jurors told the following story:—William solemnly and at the church
door espoused one Alice and they lived together as
husband and wife for sixteen years. He had several
sons and daughters by her; one of them is still
alive; his name is Richard and he is four years old.
After this there came a woman called Joan, whom
William had carnally known a long time ago, and
on whom he had begotten a child called Richard, and
she demanded William as her husband in the Court
Christian, relying on an affidation that had taken
place between them; and she, having proved her
case, was adjudged to him by the sentence of the
court and a divorce was solemnly celebrated between him and Alice. And so William and Joan
lived together for a year and more. But, said the
jurors,—sensible laymen that they were—we doubt
which of the two Richards is heir, whether Richard,
son of Joan, who is twenty-four years old, or Richard, son of Alice, who is four years old, for Joan
was never solemnly married at the door of the
church, and we say that, if neither of them is heir,
then William's brother will inherit. When this verdict came into the chancery, the attention of the
royal officers must have been pointedly drawn to
the question that we have been discussing, and, had
they thought only of their master's interests, they
would have decided in favor of Alice's son and so
secured a long wardship for the king; but, true to
the law of the church and the law of the land, they
ordered that Joan's son should have siesn of his
father's land: in other words, they preferred the
unsolemnized to the solemnized marriage.'"[15]

---

[15]History of English Law, Bk. II, p. 379.

CHAPTER V

MARRIAGE IN THE AMERICAN COLONIES

We have seen that irregular marriages were valid in England by the common law until the passage of the Act of 1753. We now come to the United States. One might suppose, in view of the fact that many of our states still recognize as valid informal marriages, that from the earliest period in the history of our country no formality was required to create the marriage relation. One learned writer says that during the eighteenth century, at least, by the prevailing law of New England, the state of matrimony could not be constituted without the intervention of a minister of the gospel, or a civil magistrate.[1]

In a summary of his chapter on The Family in The American Colonies, Goodsell says:

> "A review of colonial legislation with respect to marriage gives clear evidence that the first settlers made every attempt to safeguard the institution of matrimony and to prevent thoughtless persons from entering into the contract carelessly and without due formality. Parental consent, given to the town or county clerk personally or in writing, was everywhere required; due notice of the marriage by banns or posting or, in default of banns, by license from the Governor, was demanded in all the colonies; the solemnization of marriage was regulated by law; and, finally, registration of the marriage in town or county clerk's office, or, in colonies where the Church of England was established, by the parish clerk, was a universal requirement. In none

[1]Frank Gaylord Cook, 61 Atl. Monthly (1888). This statement, however, is disputed by Howard as will be seen elsewhere in this chapter.

54

of the colonies was "self-marriage" (incorrectly called common law marriage) in which the parties took each other for husband and wife without the presence of a magistrate or clergyman sanctioned by law. Even in Pennsylvania the law of 1693 required that one of the twelve witnesses to the ceremony should be a justice of the peace. In all the other colonies marriage by magistrate or clergyman, or (in the frontier districts of Virginia) by a layman licensed by the courts was inflexibly demanded by law. Yet there can be little doubt that "self marriage," contrary to legal provisions, did occur from time to time throughout the colonies. In such cases, except where the law expressly declared the marriage void, the offenders were liable to punishment for contracting an *illegal* marriage, but their union was not declared *invalid*. Thus the old mediæval distinction between marriages contracted contrary to law and those which were null and void from the beginning seems to have crept into colonial practice. Even in the colonies where illegal marriages were also declared invalid the statute was probably itself invalid because not in accordance with the laws of England."[2]

The foregoing summary of Goodsell is based largely on Howard's much larger work. Howard says:

"The doctrine that an informal marriage *per verba de præsenti* is valid unless expressly declared void by 'words of nullity' in the statute is not an invention of the American courts. It is the doctrine maintained by the English judges previous to the decision in the case of the Queen v. Millis in 1844; and from the evidence already presented it seems certain, if indeed it be not demonstrated, that it was the accepted doctrine in the English colonies. According to an able writer, the colonial statutory system entirely superseded the common law; and this system has been 'destroyed' by a revolution, effected through the decisions of the American

[2]The Family as a Social and Educational Institution, p. 376.

courts, 'which has introduced into our law much of
the insecurity, the irreverance, the license, of the
Middle Ages,' our common law today being 'the
canon law that existed prior to the Council of
Trent.' No doubt our common law marriage is
thoroughly bad, involving social evils of the most
dangerous character; *and no doubt the colonial
legislative system was a remarkable advance upon
anything which had elsewhere appeared.* But the
common-law marriage was not introduced by the
American judges; nor is it historically correct to
say that in the English colonies it had been entirely
supplanted by legislation, however admirable in its
intent and quality that legislation may have been.
For the colonial period, as elsewhere shown, the
relation of the statutes governing marriage to the
common law can only partially be determined from
the court records. In the southern colonies the
judicial history of the subject is almost a complete
blank.'"[3]

It is argued that many of the colonial marriage laws
were not mandatory and therefore did not supersede the
common law and for this reason Howard says history is
on the side of Chief Justice Kent. The question may
be asked, however: "Why did the colonists legislate at
all regarding the marriage celebration? Is it not significant that the mother country was passing no such
laws at that time?

After all, our present concern is not so much with the
nice distinction between illegality and invalidity which
is alleged to have existed in regard to colonial marriage
laws, but rather with the attitude the colonists, or the
majority of them, took in regard to informal marriages.
Not one instance has been shown where a marriage purely

---

[3]History of Mat. Institutions, Vol. 3, p. 170. The able writer referred
to is Cook.

per verba de præsenti without cohabitation or *per verba de futuro cum copula* was recognized in the colonies. It is not unlikely that these distinctions were unknown to them. And Howard has abundantly shown that these marriages were unpopular.[4] The fact that some of the colonies did declare such marriages null and void for all purposes but that such laws are not *laws* because not in accordance with the laws of England concerns us little. The books are full of colonial laws not in accordance with the laws of England. Moreover, after the English yoke was thrown off we jettisoned a large part of the English law as not applicable to our institutions and government. We could easily have rejected the canon law doctrine of informal marriages, which doctrine had been dead in England for a quarter of a century. At the time it was accepted there were statutes prescribing other methods of celebration. It would have been an easy matter to have declared that these statutes superseded the common law as the Supreme Court of Massachusetts did.[5]

In a note to the third edition of Reeve's Domestic Relations appears the following statement in regard to the English Marriage Act of 1753:

"This statute was enacted in 1752, but it can hardly be pretended, that, although it was passed

---

[4]History Matrimonial Institutions, Vol. II, p. 209.

[5]Professor Lorenzen says the colonists brought with them the English law of marriage and accepted the then prevailing view that marriages *per verba de præsenti* were valid. He argues that a comparison of conditions in England and the colonies would lead to the conclusion that stronger reasons existed for marriage by proxy in this country than in England. A study of the marriage laws of the colonies shows that, the colonists looked with extreme disfavor upon marriages constituted by a mere exchange of consent. 32 Harvard Law Review 482 (March, 1919).

while we were colonists of Great Britain, *as the principles upon which it was founded are so entirely hostile to the spirit of our institutions,* that it could ever be held to extend here by construction.''

This statement was first made by Justice Woodbury in 1820.[6] It is well known that the Act of 1753 was *not made applicable* to the colonies but was the English Act hostile to the spirit of our institutions? Perhaps it was in so far as it prescribed a ceremony in the Established Church. Let us now examine the colonial laws on the subject.

The laws of the Colony of New Plymouth, 1636, provided, in regard to marriage, the following:

"That none be allowed to marry that are under the covert of parents but by their consent and approbation; but in case consent cannot be had, then it shall be with the consent of the Governor or some assistant to whom the persons are known, whose care it shall be to see the marriage be fit before it be allowed by him, and after approbation be three several times published before the solemnizing of it. Or else in places where there are no such meetings that contracts or agreements of marriage may be so published that then it shall be lawful to publish them by a writing thereof made and set upon the usual public places for the space of fifteen days, provided that the writing be under some magistrate's hand or by his order.''

The laws of 1638 provided:

"Whereas divers persons unfit for marriage both in regard to their young years as also in regard to their weak estate, some practicing the inveigling of men's daughters and maids under guardians contrary to their parents' and guardians' liking, and of maid servants without leave and liking of their

---

[6]Londonderry v. Chester, 2 N. H. 268.

masters. It is, therefore, enacted by the Court that if any shall make any motion of marriage to any man's daughter or maid servant not having first obtained leave and consent of parents or master so to do, shall be punished either by fine or corporal punishment, or both, at the discretion of the bench and according to the nature of the offense.

"It is also enacted that if a motion of marriage be duly made to the minister, and through any sinister end or covetous desire he will not consent thereunto, then the cause to be made known unto the magistrate, and they be set down such order therein upon examination of the case shall appear to be most equal on both parties.'"[7]

The laws of 1639 provided:

"And for prevention of *unlawful* marriages; it is ordered that no person shall be joined in marriage, before the intention of the parties proceeding therein has been published three times at some public meeting, in the towns where the parties or either of them do ordinarily reside, or be set up in writing upon some post of their meeting house door in public view, there to stand as it may be easily read, by the space of fourteen days.[8]

The laws of 1646 provided:

"As the ordinance of marriage is honorable among all, so should it be accordingly solemnized; it is, therefore, ordered that no person in this jurisdiction shall join any persons together in marriage but the magistrate or such other as the court shall authorize in such place where no magistrate is near, *nor shall any join themselves in marriage* but before some magistrate or person authorized as aforesaid, nor shall any magistrate or other person to be au-

---

[7]The Compact with the Charter and Laws of the Colony of New Plymouth (Boston, 1836).

[8]Charters and Laws of Mass. 1628 to 1779, p. 151 (Boston, 1814). To facilitate their reading, the writer has modernized the spelling in quoting Colonial Statutes.

thorized, join or suffer any to join together in marriage in their presence before such persons' publication according to law.[9]

The laws of 1647 contain most interesting provisions in regard to marriage. All married persons who are not living with their families are directed to go back to their families at once because of the temptations under which they now live. The Act of May, 1647, provides:

"Sec. 4. Whereas divers persons, both men and women, living within this jurisdiction, whose wives and husbands are in England, or elsewhere, by means whereof, they live under great temptations here, and some of them committing lewdness and filthiness here amongst us, others make love to women and attempt marriage, and some have attained it, and some of them live under suspicion of uncleanness, and all to the great dishonor of God, reproach of religion, Commonwealth and Churches; It is therefore ordered by this Court and authority thereof, for the prevention of all such future evils, that all such married persons as aforesaid, shall repair to their said relations by the first opportunity of shipping, upon the pain or penalty of twenty pounds, except they can shew just cause to the contrary to the next county court, or Court of Assistants, after they are summoned by the constable there to appear, who are hereby required so to do, upon pain of twenty shillings for every such default wittingly made: Provided this order do not extend to such as are come over to make way for their families, or are in a transient way only for traffick or merchandise for some small time."

The Code of 1650 of Connecticut contains the following provision as to marriage:

"For as much as many persons entangle themselves with rash and inconsiderate contracts for

---

[9] *Ibid.*

their future joinage in marriage covenant, to the most trouble and grief of themselves and their friends, for the preventing thereof;

"It is ordered by the authority of this Court, That whosoever intend to join themselves in marriage covenant, shall cause their purpose of contract to be published in some public place and at some public meeting in the several towns where such persons dwell at the least eight days before they enter into such a contract whereby they engage themselves each to the other; and that they shall forbear to join in marriage covenant at least eight days after the said contract.

By the general laws revised and published by order of the general court held at Hartford in October, 1672, there is the following provision:

"For the preventing of *unlawful* marriages, it is ordered by the authority of this court that after the publication hereof no persons shall be joined in marriage before the intentions of the parties proceeding therein hath been published sufficiently at some public lecture or town meeting in the towns where the parties or either of them do ordinarily reside, or be set up in writing fairly written upon some post of their meeting house door in public view, there to stand so as it may be read eight days before such marriage."[10]

As regards Connecticut, Swift's System of Laws, published in 1795, after reciting that only ministers and magistrates are empowered to solemnize marriage, states: "An erroneous opinion has prevailed that any person not a minister or justice of the peace may join persons in marriage, but this opinion is clearly against law."[11]

---

[10]Laws of Conn. Colony, p. 46 (Samuel Green, Cambridge, 1672).

[11]Common law marriages were probably never valid in Conn. *In re* Sarah A. Bartlett, 15 Pension Dec., 290.

Among the laws passed by the General Assembly of New Hampshire, March 16, 1679, is the following:

> "For prevention of *unlawful* marriages; it is ordered that no person shall be joined in marriage, before the intention of the parties proceeding therein, have been three times published at some public meeting, in the town where the parties or either of them do ordinarily reside; or be set up in writing upon some posts of their meeting-house door in public view, there to stand, so as it may be easily read, by the space of fourteen days."[12]

By the Maryland Act of 1658 it is enacted that "all persons who shall desire marriage have liberty to apply themselves either to a magistrate or minister for the contracting thereof." The Act of 1700 provides: "And to prevent any lay persons from joining any persons in marriage where any minister or priest can be had; and to ascertain what shall be paid for marriages; Be it likewise enacted by the authority aforesaid, that in every parish where any minister or incumbent shall reside, and have charge of souls therein, no justice or magistrate, being a layman, shall join any person in marriage, under the penalty of five thousand pounds of tobacco for such offense, to our sovereign Lord the King, as aforesaid."[13] By an Act of the Houses of Assembly of Maryland passed June 8, 1717 which is entitled: "An Act for the publication of Marriages and to Prevent Unlawful Marriages," it is provided that all persons who desire marriage shall apply themselves to a minister for the contracting thereof and shall cause due publication to be made according to

---

[12]Laws of N. H., Province Period, Vol. I, p. 26.
[13]Laws of the Province of Md., 1692-1718 and May, 1719, "collected into one *volumn*," Phila. (1718).

the Rubric of the Church of England of their intention
to marry. A penalty is provided against persons marrying without publication, the penalty being a fine of five
thousand pounds of tobacco.[14]

In Maryland there was religious toleration from the
beginning. Lord Baltimore and some of his followers
were Catholics but the majority were Protestants.
Therefore, a policy of complete toleration was the only
one that could assure the Proprietary and his Catholic
followers the enjoyment of their own faith. Accordingly,
in spite of the charter, providing for the establishment
of the Church of England, such a policy was instituted.
This induced Puritans in large numbers from Virginia
and elsewhere. They soon gained control and in 1649
the Catholics found it necessary to obtain the Toleration
Act, virtually an agreement by the Council and the Assembly not to persecute Catholics. There was from the
beginning a struggle for supremacy between the Episcopacy on the one hand and Catholicism and Quakerism
on the other. Because of this fact the early marriage
laws were liberal. However, at the close of the seven-
teenth century the Episcopacy asserted itself and the
civil celebration alone maintained and it continues to
this day. A careful study of the Colonial marriage laws
of Maryland shows that religious toleration was not due
so much to Calvert's ideas of religious liberty as it was
to his desire to make secure his own religion. He was
a most liberal and broadminded man to be sure, but it
seems unlikely that had he had unlimited power he would

---

[14]Laws of Md. at Large, 2 and 3 Chas. Lord Baltimore, 1717, Ch. XV.
(Annapolis, Jonas Green, 1755. No paging in this volume).

5

have instituted a purely civil ceremony, something prohibited in every Catholic country since 1563.[15]

Referring to the early marriage laws of Maryland the
Supreme Court of Maryland said in 1872 in a case re-
jecting the English law:

> "It is true, the Act contains no express prohibi-
> tion or declaration of absolute nullity of marriages
> contracted *per verba de præsenti;* but it is plainly
> to be perceived that such marriages, if allowed,
> would contravene the spirit and policy of the Act.
> The implications from the provisions of the Act are
> exceedingly strong against such marriages, and the
> practice and custom of the people of the state have
> been so universally in conformity with what would
> appear to have been the policy and requirement
> of the law, that such custom has acquired the force
> and sanction of law, even though a question could
> be made as to the technical construction of the Act
> itself."[16]

A colonial law of Virginia 1661-1662 provided "that
no marriage be solemnized nor reputed valid in law but
such as is made by the ministers according to the laws
of England." In an Act passed by the General Assembly
of Virginia in 1748, to be effective June 10, 1751, entitled, "An Act concerning marriage," it was provided
that no person shall be married without license or publication of banns.[17] It was not until 1780 that a law was
passed providing that the ceremony might be performed
by a dissenting clergyman.

On February 22, 1785, the General Assembly of the

---

[15]See Cook, 61 Atlantic Monthly, p. 357.

[16]Dennison v. Dennison, 35 Md. 380.

[17]Acts of Assembly now in force in the Colony of Va., p. 333 (Williams-
burg, 1752).

State of Georgia passed an act which began: "And whereas divers persons have been married, by Justices of the Peace, and Ministers or Preachers of the Gospel," and then proceeds to validate them. This would indicate that informal marriages before that time were looked upon as invalid. Howard says, however, this a rash inference.[18] The Act provided:

> "Be it therefore enacted, that such marriages as have been heretofore contracted by any person or persons, before or by such justice, or minister or preacher of the gospel, are hereby ratified, confirmed and allowed as valid in law, from the time of the solemnization thereof; and all justices of the peace duly qualified, ministers or preachers of the gospel in the state regularly ordained, shall, and they are hereby empowered and authorized, after public notice of eight days being given, or by license of his honor the governor, or register of probates, to marry any person or persons enabled to enter into marriage contract: And if any such justice, or minister or preacher of the gospel, shall marry any couple without such notice, or authorized by license from the governor, or register of probates, to do so, he shall on conviction, forfeit five hundred pounds sterling, for the use of the state."

The foregoing is the earliest record of marriage legislation in Georgia that can be found.[19]

By an Act passed January 29, 1790, by the General Assembly of the State of Delaware, the preamble of which condemned the "unadvised, clandestine, loose and unseemly proceedings in marriage which tend to introduce a contempt and irreverent regard for that holy institu-

---

[18]History Matrimonial Institutions, Vol. III, p. 174.
[19]Colonial Records of Georgia, Vol. XIX, p. 458; also Watkins' Digest of the Laws of Georgia 1755-1799 p. 314 (Phila. 1800).

tion, and a dissoluteness of manner among the thoughtless part of the community," it was provided that no minister shall marry without license or publication of banns.[20]

The Code of Laws adopted by the General Assembly, of what is now Rhode Island, in 1647 provides:

> "It is agreed and ordered by the authority of the present assembly, for the preventing many evils and mischiefs that may follow thereon, that no contract or agreement between a man and a woman to own each other as man and wife, shall be owned from henceforth throughout the whole colony as a lawful marriage, nor their issue so coming together to be legitimate or lawfully begotten, but such as are in the first place with the parent's consent, then orderly published in two several meetings of the townsmen, and lastly confirmed before the head officer of the town and entered into the town clerk's book."[21]

The "Fundamental Constitutions" of 1669, granted to the Colony of North Carolina, provide that "no marriage shall be lawful, whatever contract and ceremony they have used, till both parties mutually own it before the register of the place where they were married, and he register it, with the names of the father and mother of each party." It was enacted by the first Assembly that a marriage might be celebrated by declaration before the Governor or one of the Council and three of four witnesses. In 1741 the General Assembly passed an Act

---

[20]Laws of Delaware, Vol. II p. 972 (Newcastle 1797). The Supreme Court of Delaware has held, since this work was written, that a common law marriage is not valid in Delaware because the history of the State's legislation from Colonial times shows the people endeavored to prevent such marriages. This is the first decision in this country based on this ground. (Wilmington Trust Co. v. Hendrixson 114 Atl. 215.)

[21]Proceedings of the First General Assembly, etc. Staples, (Providence, 1847).

concerning marriages which provides how and by whom a ceremony is to be performed and the fees for the same but no provision is directed against marriages entered into in any other way. It is significant, however, that the preamble reads: "For preventing clandestine and unlawful marriages."[22]

In South Carolina by the Church Act of 1704 it is provided that "no justice or magistrate, being a layman, shall presume to join any persons in marriage, under penalty of one hundred pounds current money of this Province." In 1712 it is enacted that marriages are to stand "notwithstanding pre-contracts" which is identical with the Act passed in the reign of Henry VIII and soon repealed by Parliament.

The New Jersey law of 1668 was substantially that of New England. Her law of 1682 provided: "that marriage must be solemnized by or before some justice of the peace or other magistrate within the Province, unless the justice of the peace or magistrate refuse to be present." In 1718 an act was passed entitled "An Act to prevent Clandestine Marriages." In 1795 a law was passed making a ceremony necessary.[23]

Under the laws in force in New Netherlands marriage could be effected only after due publication of banns. These laws were very stringent as is seen from "An ordinance of the director and Council of New Netherlands regulating the publication of banns of matrimony," passed January 19, 1654; also an ordinance passed Jan-

---

[22]Laws North Carolina, (Swann 1752) p. 127.

[23]If the parties ask the officer to appear and he refuses it would appear that they might marry themselves but this did not last.

uary 15, 1658, providing "that persons whose banns have been published, shall have their marriages solemnized within one month after, or show cause to the contrary" and "no man or woman shall live together as married persons, unless they are lawfully married."[24]

In 1664 New Netherlands came into the control of the English, Charles II, granting the territory to the Duke of York. The marriage laws of the Duke were not materially changed. By the Act concerning marriages passed by the first session of the legislature, October 23, 1684, it is provided:

> "Whereas by the law of England no marriage is lawfully consummated without a minister whose office is to join the parties in matrimony after the banns thrice published in the church or a license first had and obtained from some other person thereunto authorized[25] all which formality cannot be duly practiced in these parts, yet to the end a *decent* rule may be therein observed be it enacted by the General Assembly and by the authority of the same that from henceforth the names and surnames of each party who intend marriage shall be publicly read in the parish church or usual meeting place where they both then inhabit three several Lord's days together or where no church or public meeting place shall happen to be a publication in writing shall be fixed fourteen days before marriage on the door of the constable of each parish where the parties inhabit unless they bring or produce a license under the hand and seal of the Governor.
>
> "Be it further enacted by the authority that if anyone shall presume to marry contrary to the law prescribed the person offending shall be proceeded against as for fornication and the minister or jus-

---

[24]Laws and Ordinances of New Netherland. (Albany 1868.)
[25]This preamble is significant.

tice that married them shall forfeit twenty pounds and be suspended from his benefice and office.''[26]

By the Laws Agreed Upon in England, for Pennsylvania, May 5, 1682, it is provided that all marriages (not forbidden by the law of God, as to nearness of blood and affinity) shall be encouraged; but the parents or guardians shall be first consulted, and the marriage shall be published before it be solemnized, and it shall be solemnized by taking one another as husband and wife before credible witnesses, and a certificate of the whole, under the hands of parents and witnesses, shall be brought to the proper registry of that county, and shall be registered in his office. The number of witnesses required is twelve. A later statute required that one of the witnesses should be a justice of the peace. In a law enacted by the Assembly in December, 1683, the preamble reads: ''To prevent clandestine, loose and unseemly proceedings in marriage,'' but is otherwise similar to the Act of 1682.

Since this work was first written the Supreme Court of Delaware has upheld the very contention made in this chapter. In the case of Wilmington Trust Co. v. Henrixson, decided June 2, 1921, (114 Atl. 215), the court held a common law marriage was not valid in Delaware, notwithstanding a provision of the code which reads: ''Nothing in this chapter contained shall be deemed or taken to render any common-law or other marriage, otherwise lawful, invalid by reason of failure to take out a license as herein provided.'' The court held that this was a mere recital, that is, that a common law marriage

---

[26]Colonial Laws of New York 1664 to the Revolution, Vol. I, p. 150 Albany, 1894.

is a marriage otherwise lawful, and not a positive legislative declaration recognizing such marriages. The court
further held that common law marriage is contrary to
the spirit of American institutions as evidenced by our
Colonial history and policy, and therefore refused to
adopt it as a part of the common law of Delaware. This
decision is not yet published but Chief Justice Pennewill
has been kind enough to supply me with a copy of his
decision. Because of the importance of this case, the
following extracts are taken from the opinion, eliminat-
ing the authorities quoted in support thereof:

"As we understand the arguments, the contentions of the
plaintiff may be summarized as follows:

(1) That the facts agreed upon in the case stated show there
was a marriage between the parties, good at common law.

(2) That at common law an informal or nonceremonial marriage was valid if there was an agreement *per verba de præsenti*
betwen the parties that they would live together as husband and
wife; and that there was such an agreement in this case.

(3) That the common law of England was adopted by this
State, and that part of it which related to marriage became the
law of this State, and was such at the time the marriage in question was consummated.

(4) That while the statutes of this State have directed how
marriages should be performed and have gone so far as to declare when they shall be valid, no statute has ever declared that
a common law, or nonceremonial marriage shall be void or invalid.

(5) That practically every State in this country having statutes substantially similar to ours and in which there is no statute
making such marriages invalid, has recognized them as valid.

(6) That our present marriage law expressly recognizes such marriages as valid by providing that nothing therein contained shall be deemed or taken to render any common law or other marriage, otherwise lawful, invalid by reason of the failure to take out a license as is therein provided.

The contentions of the defendants are:

(1) That the common law respecting marriages was never adopted in this State.

(2) That even if it was, the marriage in question was not a good marriage at common law because not contracted by words of present consent.

(3) That a nonceremonial marriage was not good at common law.

(4) That while a large majority of the States of this country have seen fit to recognize a common law or nonceremonial marriage there are some that have not, and reason as well as sound policy require that our State should not recognize such a marriage.

(5) That the legislation of this State, while not expressly declaring such a marriage void or illegal, nevertheless, through its entire history unmistakably shows that only a ceremonial marriage is valid, and by the strongest kind of implication declares that a common law or nonceremonial marriage is invalid.

In this State it has been held that the common law of England is in force only so far as it has been adopted in practice, and so far as concerns our condition and circumstances.

It is argued that when this State had covered the subject of marriage by legislation, and such legislation was inconsistent with the common law, it cannot be held that the common law respecting marriages has ever been adopted in practice, or was adapted to our circumstances and conditions.

It is undoubtedly true that the legislation of this State representing marriage fully covers the subject, and shows by the strongest implication, at least, that the common law, so far as it relates to marriage, was not favored or applicable. We are of the opinion, therefore, that such common law has never been adopted in this State.

If the history of the State's legislation is carefully considered, it will be found that from colonial times private, loose or clandestine marriages have not only been discouraged, but the effort has been to prevent them. Statutes have been enacted for the express purpose of preventing "clandestine marriages." Our marriage law makes void a marriage solemnized by a person having no authority in that behalf unless one of the parties believed it was lawful.

And so, it is manifest from the history of marriage legislation in this State that a secret, clandestine or nonceremonial marriage was never intended to be valid. The law has at no time contemplated that it should be recognized. If a marriage entered into without any publicity or ceremony at all must be valid, why should there be any law prescribing how a marriage shall be consummated or what shall constitute a legal marriage?

Our conclusion is that no matter what marriage statutes and their judicial interpretation in other States may be, a fair construction of our own statutes makes a secret and nonceremonial marriage illegal and void. And we base our conclusion on the apparent meaning and object of legislation on the subject, as well as upon the manifest policy of the State. To make a good legal marriage something more is required than cohabitation and repute. Even a secret agreement to live together as husband and wife, and a reputation as such among neighbors, and friends, will not make it a valid marriage.

It is impossible to escape the conclusion that many courts in this country have construed marriage laws very liberally because, as the Rhode Island court expressed it, "to make marriage void and children illegitimate, by implication, is a serious thing."

The desire to make the offspring of informal marriages legitimate is, of course, commendable, and legalizing such marriages would be equally so if they were entered with an honest intent by either party, that is, with the belief that the marriage was lawful. *But unfortunately such intent or belief is exceedingly rare.* Usually in such marriages the relation in the beginning is nothing other than licentious, and the question is whether the interests of the innocent children of such unions are paramount to the good of society. We know it is essential in a nonceremonial marriage that there shall be an agreement in the beginning that the parties assume the relation of husband and wife; they must presently agree they will live together as such. But the trouble is that such agreement can rarely be shown except by their conduct, and there is no perceptible difference in this regard between innocent and guilty conduct. Hardly ever do parties to such relation declare their purpose or intent in the beginning, and, therefore, it must be shown by circumstances, that is, by their conduct—cohabitation.

And the recognition of informal marriages to make innocent children legitimate may be attended with unfortunate results in many cases. Suppose, for example, that after continued cohabitation, and reputation as married people, and after children are born, there comes, as in the present case, separation of the parents, and either party contracts a similar marriage with another person and raises children, what will be the status of the innocent offspring of the later union? There cannot be two valid marriages. To put a more extreme and difficult case, suppose after the separation, either party contracts a marriage in a perfectly legal manner and raises children. What would be the situation of the parent and the children?

It seems, therefore, that legalizing an informal marriage so that the children shall be legitimate may cause troubles and complications of a very serious character to parents, children and society. It is the opinion of the court that the legislature having dealt intelligently, carefully and fully with the subject of marriage and having declared what shall institute a legal marriage, the court may assume that a marriage contracted otherwise is unlawful and invalid. If the law works a hardship in any case upon parent or child, there is an obvious and practicable remedy, viz. An application to the Legislature to validate the marriage and legitimize the children.

It would be, we take it, nothing short of shocking to our people if the court should in this day of easy marriage and frequent divorce hold that a secret, clandestine or informal marriage is valid in this State. Even if the question of the validity of such a marriage was a doubtful one, the interests of innocent children would have to be weighed against the protection of the community and the good of society. We are not inclined to make marriages more easy or divorces more frequent than they are, and upon the whole question our minds are clear that what is called a common law marriage is invalid. As already said, the safest and wisest course, for the correction of any wrong or relief of any hardship is to apply to the Legislature, which may, and doubtless will in any proper case, by specific act validate a marriage which, under general law, is invalid.

Some of the States in which the courts have recognized non-ceremonial or common law marriages because their laws did not expressly make them invalid *have since made them invalid by express statutory provision.* No doubt this was done in obedience to what the law-making bodies conceived to be sound reason and wise public policy under existing conditions; and it is difficult to escape the belief that many courts that have held such marriages good might be of a different opinion today if the question was a new one. But while we know that the good of society requires that a marriage, to be valid, should be something more than the mere agreement of the parties to live together, we base our conclusion on the obvious meaning of the Legislature of our own State on the subject.

We are clearly of the opinion that a common law or a non-ceremonial marriage entered into in this State is not a valid marriage.

CHAPTER VI

EARLY AMERICAN DECISIONS FOR AND AGAINST COMMON LAW MARRIAGE

The earliest reported case involving the question of common law marriage is the Maryland case of Cheseldine v. Brewer decided in 1739. (1. H. & McH. 152.) Howard in his work on Matrimonial Institutions cites this case to show that common law marriages were recognized in the colonies. He also says Justice Alvey's statement in the Maryland case of Dennison v. Dennison (decided in 1873) that the laws of that state never sanctioned common law marriage cannot be considered as decisive, citing this case. It sems strange indeed, as has been elsewhere pointed out, that a man of Justice Alvey's ability would make such an error with regard to the law of his own state. The case is indexed only under the head ''What is sufficient *proof* of marriage to render issue legitimate.'' It is quite possible that the case involved only the evidence necessary to *prove* a marriage and not the question whether marriage *per verba de præsenti* or *per verba de futuro* was legal in Maryland. The brief report of the case lends color to this view. The report of the case follows in full:

> ''This was an ejectment for a tract of land called Matapany. At the Assises held for St. Mary's County, at the trial of the cause, the plaintiff, to prove that he was the legitimate son and heir of Kenelm Cheseldine, his reputed father, and through whom he claimed title to the land in question as his

heir at law, offered evidence, that Kenelm Cheseldine, cohabited with Mary Sheppard, the mother of
the plaintiff, from the year 1712 to the time of his
death, which happened in the year 1717; and that
during that time the said Kenelm and Mary, had
often declared that he was married to the said
Mary, and he that she was his lawful wife, except
at some particular times, when intoxicated or in a
passion; that the plaintiff was born in the year
1712, sometime after the cohabitation had com-
menced, and that the said Kenelm owned him for
his son. The defendant prayed the justices to declare to the jury, that the evidence was not sufficient
to prove the lessor of the plaintiff to be the legitimate son of Kenelm Cheseldine, his supposed father, as no actual marriage was proved. But the
justices directed the jury, that if they found the said
Kenelm and Mary had consented and agreed to be
man and wife, and had cohabited and copulated as
such before the birth of the lessor of the plaintiff,
that they should render their verdict for the plaintiff. To this direction of the court the defendant
excepted. And this court affirmed the judgment.''

Perhaps the earliest case involving the question in
this county after our independence is Mangue v. Mangue,
(1 Mass. 240-1804) in which case the doctrine was not
recognized. This was a libel for divorce on the ground
of adultery. To prove the marriage the plaintiff offered
in evidence a certificate of a justice of the peace as
follows:

"Be it remembered that on the 17th day of......
came before me J. B. one of the Justices of the
Peace for the county of........Henry Mangue and
Nancy Neale, when the said Henry Mangue took the
said Nancy Neale by her right hand and voluntarily
said, I take this Nancy Neale to be my wedded wife,
and I promise to do for and conduct towards her in
all respects according to the rules of the marriage
covenant so long as it shall please God to continue

us both in this life—and then let go her right hand—
when the said Nancy Neale immediately took the
said Henry Mangue by his right hand, and voluntarily said, (repeating the words before used,
mutatis mutandis), of which proceedings as aforesaid the said Henry Mangue and Nancy Neale required of me the said Justice to make record, and
called upon one S. N. and B. S., then present, to bear
witness to the whole of their proceedings.''
S. N.
B. S.   Before me, J. B., Justice of the Peace.''

And it appeared that each party signed and left in the
hands of the justice, a writing by which they acknowledged the transactions above mentioned to have taken
place, viz., ''I take this Nancy Neale to be my wedded,
etc.'' as above recited.

The court refused to grant the divorce on the ground
that there was no marriage to dissolve. The brief opinion
of one of the justices reads:

''Here is no evidence of a marriage—no such evidence as is known in law—the parties agreed to
come together, and they may now agree to separate.''

CHAPTER VII

THE DEVELOPMENT OF COMMON LAW MARRIAGE IN THE UNITED STATES

We have seen that purely consensual marriages were never affirmatively recognized in the colonies; that such marriages were abolished in England prior to the American Revolution; and that in England the question has, perhaps, been the subject of as much debate as has any one subject in the law. Then, how do we account for the present American doctrine in view of the fact that practically every state has a statute prescribing the form of celebration of marriage? Are we to find some great early American decisions on the question? No, not one.

The doctrine of the common law marriage, so called, was given an impetus in this country by Chancellor Kent in 1809. In a dictum in the case of Fenton v. Reed, followed by a declaration to the same effect in his Commentaries, Chancellor Kent established a rule which was adopted here and there *without question* until in a large number of the states marriage is regarded as a civil contract merely, to be entered into by mutual consent as any other contract.

Fenton v. Reed, 4 Johns. (N. Y.) 52, (1809). The opinion in this case covers but one half a page and no mention is made of the Massachusetts case decided in 1804, or the Maryland case. The plaintiff claimed to be the widow of one Reed. Her first husband, Guest, deserted her in 1785. Believing Guest was dead, she married Reed in 1792. Guest did not die until 1800. But the plaintiff continued to live with Reed as his wife until 1806 when he died. It was held, *Per Curiam*,[1] that "no formal solemnization of marriage was requisite. A contract of marriage *per verba de præsenti* amounts to an actual marriage and is as valid as if made in *facie ecclesiæ* (6 Mod. 155; 2 Salk. 437; Peake's Cases, 231).[2] In the present case there existed strong circumstances from which a marriage subsequent to the death of Guest might be presumed. * * * A jury would have been warranted, under the circumstances of this case, to have inferred an actual marriage, and the court below had sufficient grounds to draw that conclusion; and as they have drawn it, and their decision being a substitute for a verdict, we will not disturb it."

So much of this opinion as relates to a marriage *per verba de præsenti* is *obiter dictum*. The opinion is otherwise unsatisfactory as a precedent. All it decides is that the evidence is sufficient to infer an actual marriage. We can only conjecture what the decision would have been had the plaintiff denied any marriage other than *per verba de præsenti*.

One writer on this subject, says, referring to this case and the dictum as to marriages *per verba de præsenti*:

> "This statement was an *obiter dictum;* and, as usually interpreted it would seem hardly to have been borne out by the English cases cited. In fact, this doctrine was novel to American courts. It was also inconsistent with the statutory system that had

---

[1] There is good reasons for believing Kent wrote the opinion.

[2] It is interesting to observe that no American authority is cited in support of this statement. There is absolutely no discussion of the earlier American marriage laws.

come down from colonial times,—especially with that system as it existed in New York prior to the Revolution. Yet this case went far to settle the law of New York, and has been cited throughout this country with the spread, and in support, of the doctrine which it introduced."[3]

In 1810 the same question was put to the Supreme Court of Massachusetts in the case of Milford v. Worcester in which an opposite conclusion was reached. This case continues to be law in Massachusetts and also in a few states where the Kent doctrine has never been accepted.

Milford v. Worcester, 7 Mass. 48. The question in this case was whether the mutual engagement of Stephen Temple and Rhoda Essling, made at the tavern in Upton, under the circumstances there existing was a lawful marriage. The evidence of a marriage between the said Stephen and Rhoda was,—a certificate by the town clerk of Upton, in the county of Worcester, that in the book kept for that purpose, there is an entry July 6, 1784, of the intention of marriage of Stephen Temple and Rhoda Essling; and by the deposition of the said Rhoda, and the testimony of other witnesses, it appeared that in the year 1784, the parties came together to a tavern in Upton, when one Dorr, Esq., then a justice of the peace for the county of Worcester, happened to be there; and producing a certificate that their intentions of marriage had been published, requested him to marry them: but he, after some enquiry into the cause of the application to him, refused "to take an active part," as the witnesses expressed it. The parties continued notwithstanding in the room where the said Dorr was, and there in his presence, and before several witnesses, declared themselves husband and wife, each making to the other the vows,and promises usual in contracting marriages. Six children were born of this union. The court held that under the provincial charter in force in 1784, a marriage before a justice of the peace or minister is valid only where the justice or minister assents to the marriage, he undertaking to act on the occasion in his official capacity. It was urged that the marriage, although not solemnized pursuant to the statute, was valid because not declared void by any statute. The court, in holding the marriage void and the issue bastards, said: ''When therefore the statute enacts that no person but a justice or minister shall solemnize a marriage, and that only in certain cases, the parties are themselves prohibited from solemnizing their own marriages by any form of engagement, or in the presence of any witnesses whatever.''

It is difficult to see why one learned writer should condemn the New York case and then refer to this case as being ''decided by a jurist of distinguished learning, ability and reputation.''[4] We agree with Mr. Bishop that this opinion shows a lack of the usual research of that court. Chief Justice Parsons' statement, ''when our ancestors left England, and ever since, it is well known that a lawful marriage there must be celebrated before a clergyman in orders,'' shows he had not exhausted the subject. He cites not a case in his opinion. Howard says the opinion is ''not remarkable for historical knowledge.''[5]

---

[4] Cook, 61 Atl. Monthly.
[5] History Matrimonial Institutions, Vol. III, p. 179.

The rule was approved in a dictum of the Supreme Court of Pennsylvania in 1814, although it was not necessary for the decision in the case. In the case of Hantz v. Sealy (6 Binn. 405) an action was brought by the plaintiff against the administrator of the estate of her alleged deceased husband, to recover the amount of personal estate bequeathed to her by his last will. The plaintiff and deceased were properly married by a clergyman but the deceased had not been divorced from his former wife at the time of his second marriage. Later, however, his first wife died and his lawyer advised him to have the ceremony again performed. The deceased then said in the presence of his attorney and wife: "I take you for my wife" and she said "To be sure he is my husband good enough." The court said at page 408:

> "The defendant pleaded that he was married to the plaintiff, on which issue was joined, and it was objected that the judge ought to have directed the jury that the evidence proved the marriage. The judge laid down the law correctly. He told the jury that marriage was a civil contract, which might be completed by any words in the present time, without regard to form. He told them also that in his opinion the words proved did not constitute a marriage and in this I agree with him."

The court cited absolutely no authority for the above statement. It will be observed that this is an extreme case. A ceremony was performed but an impediment existed. The impediment was subsequently removed. The parties continued to live together. There are many cases in the reports today upholding the validity of such a marriage after the removal of the impediment. Mr.

Bishop's criticism of this decision is entirely correct.[6] The case shows that the Pennsylvania court was not eager to adopt the rule, and the proponents of common law marriage should get little inspiration from this case, yet it is always cited as authority. Singularly enough, although there are dicta in two cases that marriages by mere words in the present are valid, yet there has never been a case before the Supreme Court of Pennsylvania where the question was necessary for the decision. Marriages without ceremony have been recognized as valid by the courts of Pennsylvania since the decision in this case but there has always been cohabitation as well as words of present consent.

New Hampshire was the next state to consider this subject, in the case of Londonderry v. Chester, 2 N. H. 268, decided in 1820. In this case there was a marriage performed by a Presbyterian clergyman while he was under censure and enjoined to desist from preaching. The statute authorized only ordained ministers of the gospel and justices of the peace to celebrate marriages. The larger part of the opinion of twelve pages is taken up with a discussion of the *de facto* character of the minister. The court, however, discusses the whole subject more intelligently than has heretofore been done in America. And, although the discussion was not necessary for the deci-

---

[6]In Rose v. Clark, 8 Paige 574 (N. Y. 1841), a marriage was presumed from the mere acknowledgment of the parties that they were married, after the impediment was removed. See also Travers v. Rinehart, 96 U. S. 76; contra, dissenting opinion Holmes, J., in that case; also People v. Shaw, 259 Ill. 544. See Bishop Marriage, Divorce and Separation Vol. I, Sec. 344. The learned author of the note to Becker v. Becker, L. R. A. 1915 E p. 65 says the decision in Hantz v. Sealey is unquestionably erroneous.

sion, the common law doctrine was approved.[7] The dictum did not, however, become the settled law of New Hampshire. In 1849 in the case of Dunbarton v. Franklin, 19 N. H. 257, the court, in construing a marriage statute, less mandatory than many that have been held to be directory, which statute was in force when Londonderry v. Chester was decided, held that:

> "When laws are made, upon whatever subject, it is the duty of the citizen to conform to them. * * * The statute does not authorize persons to solemnize their own marriages, and the implied prohibition against their doing so is very strong. If such a marriage as the one in question is valid, the statute never need be regarded at all. It is entirely inoperative."

The court observed that "the remarks of Mr. Justice Woodbury in that case, although relevant to the general question, were not called for by the particular matter to be decided by the court." The court also made the following interesting observation which shows the temper of the New Hampshire court on the subject:

> "If it be important to give publicity to the contract, to guard against deception, to provide that there shall be accessible evidence of the solemnization of the contract, there is a sufficient reason for the passage of the law. All civilized nations agree that these are weighty considerations, and in all such nations, even in Scotland, where it is a sufficient solemnization of the contract to acknowledge it before witnesses, some attestation is requisite. It is singular that the most important of all human contracts, on which the rights and duties of the

---

[7]The annotator to Reeves' Domestic Relations, 3rd Ed. pays great tribute to Justice Woodbury's dictum in this case. No mention is made, however, of the fact that the decision was subsequently disapproved of and virtually overruled.

whole community depend, requires less formality for its validity than a conveyance of one acre of land, a policy of insurance, or the agreements which the statute of frauds requires should be in writing. It would be stronger still if the law should be such as to offer a temptation to illicit intercourse, where a contract lightly made could be easily repudiated, should make no provision for publicity and offer no security against fraud or undue influence. If it be once established that cohabitation and reputation constitute a marriage, the former must precede the latter. It is the cohabitation that raises the presumption and causes the reputation of matrimony. What would be easier than for the parties to agree privately that they are husband and wife, and after a cohabitation of a week or less, to separate either from incompatibility of temper or from the less worthy consideration that they have become tired of each other, or galled by even this temporary bond? Such a transformation of a penal offense into matrimony, where the alleged marriage might be dissolved, as it probably in many cases would be, by the caprice of the parties, would often follow, if, at the inception of the contract, nothing but cohabitation were required. And this temptation to illicit intercourse should be guarded against, for the sake of good morals, and has been so, as Woodbury, J. says, by our practice and the usage of most civilized nations, by requiring some form of solemnization.''

Kentucky was the next state to adopt the common law rule. In Dumaresly v. Fishly, 10 Ky. 368, (1821) a marriage license was obtained in Louisville, Kentucky and the ceremony was performed by a Catholic priest in Jeffersonville, Indiana, just across the river from Louisville. The parties never cohabited and the alleged husband slandered the wife and she brought an action to which he pleaded that he was her lawful husband. Upon this issue the Kentucky court held in favor of the husband, sustaining the marriage. The court said that neither the Indiana nor Kentucky marriage statute was mandatory and the common law rule was approved.

Judge Mills delivered a strong dissent, however, and it is the best attack on the *per verba de præsenti* rule up to this time. He insists that at common law the wife was not entitled to dower unless she proved a marriage *de jure* and that a marriage *per verba de præsenti* does not so merge her estate and identity into that of her husband as to be a defense to an action for slander; that he is not entitled to her property upon such a marriage and for a stronger reason should not be entitled to ruin her reputation; also that it was contrary to justice for the husband to denounce the marriage, slander the wife, then claim a marriage *de facto* which would entitle her not even "to the paltry *quid pro quo,* dower in his estate!" But this decision was not to remain the law of Kentucky. The legislature, evidently taking a different view from that of Justice Woodbury of New Hampshire and Reeve's Commentator, in 1852 passed a law declaring void all marriages celebrated other than in accordance with the provisions of the statute. And this statute remains in force until the present day.

The Supreme Court of Texas in a case defending Judge Mills' dissenting opinion made the following observation:

> "Besides, the marriage was entered into in the State of Indiana, and should have been determined by the law of that state. I can find no decision by the Supreme Court of Indiana that promulgates the "contract only" doctrine. (Grigsby v. Rieb, 105 Tex. 597; 153 S. W. 1124; L. R. A. 1915 E, 1.)

In 1827 Chancellor Kent published the second volume of his Commentaries. In Lecture XXVI (6) he says in regard to the forms of marriage:

> "No peculiar ceremonies are requisite by the common law to the valid celebration of the marriage. The consent of the parties is all that is required; and as marriage is said to be a contract *jure gentium,* that consent is all that is required by natural or public law. The Roman lawyers strongly inculcated the doctrine, that the very foundation and essence of the contract consisted in consent freely given by parties competent to contract. *Nihil proderit signasse tabulas, si mentem matrimonii non fuisse constabit. Nuptias non concubitas, sed consensus facit.* This is the language equally of the common and canon law, and of common reason.

> "If the contract be made *per verba de præsenti,* or if it be made *per verba de futuro,* and be followed by consummation, it amounts to a valid marriage, and which the parties (being competent as to age and consent) cannot dissolve, and it is equally binding as if made in *facie ecclesiae.* There is no recognition of any ecclesiastical authority in forming the connection, and it is considered entirely in the light of a civil contract. This is the doctrine of the common law, and also of the canon law, which governed marriages in England prior to the Marriage Act of 26 Geo. II; and the canon law is also the general law throughout Europe as to marriages, except where it has been altered by the local municipal law. The only doubt entertained by the common law was, whether cohabitation was also necessary to give validity to the contract."

The only American case Kent cites in support of the above is Fenton v. Reed which he decided in 1810.

In 1829 the subject was considered by the Supreme Court of Vermont and the rule was approved, it being held that the statute was merely directory and as the parties had lived together twenty years and reared a family of children there was sufficient evidence of marriage. The authorities cited are Kent, Reeve, Fenton v. Reed, and Londonderry v. Chester, which latter case ceased to be law in New Hampshire in 1849. The decision of 1829 was subsequently repudiated, however, in the case of Morrill v. Palmer, 68 Vt. 1 (1895), the court saying, "We hold, therefore, that what the learned commentator Kent calls the 'loose doctrine of the common law' in relation to marriage was *never* in force in this state. Thus we see the dictum in the case decided in 1829,[8] unlike the dicta in many other early cases never became law.

The question was also considered by the Supreme Court of New Jersey in 1829 in the case of Pearson v. Howey, 6 Halstead, 15. Although not necessary to the decision, Justice Ford, in a concurring opinion, strongly approves the common law rule (citing Fenton v. Reed as American authority), stating that England had lately (as a matter. of fact it was 70 years previously) repealed her old common law rule and that the innovation was "obnoxious to the country, to the wisest, and best and most virtuous men among them, as well it would seem, as to their courts of justice, and it is yet a problem whether they will not connive at the evasion of it." It would seem that this statement is hardly excusable. The innovation was objectionable only because it went to the other extreme. It is a fact that even the judges who decided in favor of the validity of these marriages in the nineteenth century disapproved of the rule. Lord Campbell, although deciding in favor of the validity of these marriages at common law says:

---

[8]The decision of 1829 referred to is Newbury v. Brunswick (2 Vt. 151).

"I have always been of opinion that to constitute this, the most important of all contracts on which society itself depends there ought to be a public form of celebration to which no reasonable person can object, admitting by means of registration, of easy, certain, and perpetual proof; the addition of a religious solemnity being highly desirable, although not absolutely necessary. (Beamish v. Beamish, p. 338.)

And Lord Stowell says that:

"in most civilized countries, acting under a sense of the force of sacred obligations, it (marriage) has had the sanctions of religion superadded * * though it is not unworthy of remark that, amidst the manifold ritual provisions made by the Divine Lawgiver of the Jews for various offices and transactions of life, there is no ceremony prescribed for the celebration of marriage." (Dalrymple case, p. 64.)[9]

The common law was approved by the Court of Appeals of South Carolina in 1832 and 1833. (Fryer v. Fryer, Rich. Eq. Cases, 85 and Jewell v. Magood, ibid. p. 113). In the first case, while the decision was against the validity of the marriage, the court approved the rule *per verba de præsenti* but criticized severely the rule *per verba de futuro,* so much so that this case has been cited as authority that the rule is not in force in that state.[10] No authority is cited, however. In the second case the decision

[9]The latter part of this statement has been seized upon by many as authority. As a matter of fact it has been shown that the family law of Israel is more primitive in type than that of Babylon or Egypt which preceded it; also that the legal system of Israel "did not stand in the forefront of the great systems of the ancient world" and that the political importance which has been attached to it is the product of reverence and imagination," due to its relation to the Christian religion. Historical Jurisprudence, Guy Carleton Lee, Johns Hopkins University, p. 95-111 (MacMillan Co. 1911.)

[10]Treas. Dept. Doc. 2834, C. L. M. in the U. S.

was also against the validity of the marriage but the court
approved both *rules* saying:

> "I had occasion to consider the subject fully, of
> what will constitute marriage in this state; cer-
> tainly, by our law, marriage is regarded only as a
> civil contract, and whatever is sufficient evidence of
> the assent of the parties' minds to enter into that
> relation, establishes a marriage. This may be either
> *per verba de præsenti*, "I take you for my wife,"
> etc., or *per verba de futuro*, an agreement to marry
> in future, with subsequent cohabitation. Where
> parties agree to marry in future, and afterwards
> cohabit, the law infers that this cohabitation was an
> execution of the previous agreement."

Certainly the latter part of this statement needs explanation. The court cited absolutely no authority.

In 1842 Greenleaf published his work on evidence. He
says:

> "Marriage is a civil contract, *jure gentium,* to the
> validity of which the consent of the parties, able to
> contract, is all that is required by natural or public
> law. If the contract is made *per verba de præsenti,*
> though it is not consummated by cohabitation, it
> amounts to a valid marriage, in the absence of all
> civil regulations to the contrary. (Citing Kent and
> Fenton v. Reed.)

Greenleaf's treatise on evidence was a great piece of
work and his statement did much to further the doctrine.
There is hardly a case on the subject during the next half-
century that doesn't cite his statement as authority. It
was not sufficient to convince the Supreme Court of the
United States in the following year, however, as we will
presently see.

The question first came before the Supreme Court of
the United States in 1843 but the court was unable to

reach a decision, being evenly divided. (Jewell v. Jewell, 1 Howard, 219.)

In 1795 Benjamin Jewell and Sophie Prevost began to live together as husband and wife. They had eight children and the mother was known as Mrs. Jewell. In 1810 they agreed to separate and executed a written agreement whereby the mother was to have three children, a number of slaves and three thousand dollars, and the father was to have five children. In 1813 Benjamin Jewell married Sarah Isaacs according to the rights and ceremonies observed by the Jews. In 1818 Sophie Prevost married one Storme. In 1828 Benjamin Jewell died intestate in Louisiana; and his widow and children brought ejectment against his children in Charleston, S. C., to recover a house and lot of which the latter were in possession.

The whole question turned on the validity of the first marriage. It appeared that Jewell was a Jew and Sophie was a Catholic; that the ceremony was performed by a man named White, in the presence of her family and other persons; that she was entirely ignorant of the English language; that they lived as husband and wife in Charleston, where he kept a clothing store; that she was recognized in society as his wife; and that the reason they did not comply fully with the law regarding ceremonial marriages was because according to the Hebrew religion a marriage between a Christian and a Jew is illegal. The case was also complicated by a release executed by Sophie in 1796, by which, in consideration of five hundred dollars, she released Jewell from an action on a promise of marriage which she had brought against him.

The circuit court, citing Kent (2 Comm. 86), instructed

the jury that ''if the contract be made *per verba de præsenti,* and remains without cohabitation, or if made *per verba de futuro,* and be followed by consummation, it amounts to a valid marriage and which the parties (being competent as to age and consent) cannot dissolve; and it is equally binding as if made in *facie ecclesiæ.''*

Upon this question the Supreme Court of the United States was evenly divided and no opinion could be given, although the case was reversed on another ground. But in 1878, as we will soon see, the Supreme Court adopted the Kent doctrine without qualification because it had already gotten a firm hold on the state courts.

Referring to the Jewell case, Peck in his work on Domestic Relations says:

> ''The very distinguished editor of the sixth edition of Kent's Commentaries (O. W. Holmes, Jr.), states that the Supreme Court of the United States was also equally divided as to the validity of a common law marriage in Jewell v. Jewell, 1 How. (U. S.) 219, but this is an error; the question was as to the local law of Georgia and South Carolina. The later cases already cited show that the view of the Supreme Court as to the doctrine of the American common law is entirely free from doubt.''[11]

It is believed by the present writer that Mr. Justice Holmes is entirely correct and this is the view of Dr. Bishop in his work on Marriage and Divorce.[12] Of course, the question depended on the local law of the states mentioned, but in Georgia the question had never been decided and the Supreme Court was asked to determine the common law of Georgia on the question. It was easy for

---

[11]Peck Dom. Rel. Page 16.
[12]Bishop Marriage, Divorce and Separation Vol. I, p. 177.

the Supreme Court to ascertain the law of South Carolina, if it in any way depended on that law, as the question had been decided there in 1832, (Rich. Eq. Cas. 85; 113). And, there is no federal common law. It is difficult to see just what Judge Peck means.

In 1852, in an opinion of less than one page in length, the Supreme Court of California, in the case of Graham v. Bennett, 2 Calif. 503, approved the Kent doctrine. No authorities are cited in the opinion. The appellee cites Kent's case (Fenton v. Reed, 4 Johns. 52) and the respondent cites the case of Chief Justice Parsons, (Milford v. Worcester, 7 Mass. 55). In this case the marriage contract was in writing and the parties lived together but the man had another wife living. The only question was whether this marriage was a void marriage for the purpose of making the children legitimate under the act which provided that the issue of void marriages shall be legitimate. The court held "the marriage legitimate in form," though void, and the children legitimate. This case, however, is not a direct decision in favor of a marriage *per verba de præsenti*. All doubt was removed by the Code of March 21, 1872, which makes solemnization or cohabitation necessary. Common law marriages are rendered entirely void by the Act of March 26, 1895.

In 1856 the High Court of Errors and Appeals of Mississippi adopted the Kent doctrine in the case of Hargroves v. Thompson, 31 Miss. 211, holding that, as the Mississippi statute did not expressly declare void, marriages not celebrated in conformity to its provisions, the facts in this case constituted a valid common law marriage, citing only Kent and Greenleaf. The facts showed that the parties had cohabited and a child was born to them. The wife died and the husband claimed her property. The administrator denied that there was a marriage. Neither this case nor the subsequent cases actually decide, however, that a marriage by mere words either *de præsenti* or *de futuro cum copula* is valid.

In 1860 the Supreme Court of Georgia considered the question in the case of Askew v. Dupree, 30 Ga. 173, and the Kent doctrine was approved. It must be observed that this opinion is the most thorough up to this time. The court accepts the Dalrymple case as the common law on the subject, (relying on Kent to a great extent) and although the Millis case is referred to, no reason is assigned for not following it other than the fact that the Dalrymple case had been followed in the past. A number of paragraphs in the opinion were taken from the Dalrymple case. As happened in nearly all these cases the court takes pains to point out that the English Marriage Act of 1753 did not apply to this country but not a word is said as to what the law of Georgia was at that time. The court says in regard to the case decided by Chief Justice Parsons:

> "And in Milford v. Worcester, 7 Mass. Rep. 48, it was held, that the parties were precluded from solemnizing their own marriage, and that a marriage by mutual agreement, not according to the statute was void. But this opinion, evidently a departure from the general doctrine [at the time the Massachusetts case was decided the general doctrine here referred to was the half-page opinion decided by Kent the previous year] and distasteful to the public sentiment [??] was overruled in the subsequent case of Parben v. Harvey, 1 Grey's Rep. 119."

7

As a matter of fact the case is Parton v. Hervey. Moreover, it did not decide anything of the kind. Milford v. Worcester continues to be the law of Massachusetts, as well as other states, to this day.

The following year, 1861, the question was considered by the Supreme Court of Ohio in the case of Carmichael v. State, 12 Ohio St. 553. In this case the person who solemnized the marriage had no license. The parties cohabited as husband and wife. The man married again without a divorce and was convicted. The conviction was affirmed. The opinion of the court, while approving the rule *per verba de præsenti,* emphasizes the fact that there was cohabitation in this case. The opinion quotes at length from the dissenting opinions in the case of Regina v. Millis.

In 1869 the Supreme Court of Alabama held that a marriage good at common law is a valid marriage in that state. (Campbell's Admr. v. Gullatt, 43 Ala. 57.) In this case the parties were married before a justice of the peace in 1862 and subsequently lived together until the death of the husband in 1869. It was alleged that the justice had no authority to issue the license. It was not necessary in this case to hold that a marriage good at common law is good in Alabama. Examination of subsequent Alabama cases shows that both of the common law rules have been rejected and cohabitation is necessary to constitute a common law marriage, even though the agreement is made *per verba de præsenti.* (Herd v. Herd, 194 Ala. 613; L. R. A. 1916B, 1243.)

In 1873 the rule was approved *obiter dictum* by the Illinois Supreme Court in the case of Port v. Port, 70 Ills.

484, which became the law of that state. The court apparently relied greatly on Bishop and the New York cases. While the court quotes from the English cases, the quotations are taken from Bishop. Had the court read the 373-page opinion of Regina v. Millis it is believed it would not have referred to the case as The King v. Millis.

In 1875 the Supreme Court of Michigan considered the question in the case of Hutchins v. Kimmell, 31 Mich. 126. Kimmell sued Hutchins for criminal conversation with Kimmell's wife. One of the defenses was that the woman was not Kimmell's wife. There was in evidence a properly authenticated certificate of marriage, showing that the parties were married by a Lutheran minister in Wurtemburg. The certificate was objected to because it was not shown that the ceremony was in accordance with the law of the country where it took place. The court, by Judge Cooley, held first, that the common law as it exists among us, will be presumed to prevail in a foreign country in the absence of proof to the contrary and second, that the facts in the case were sufficient to constitute a marriage by the common law of Michigan.

In 1876 the Supreme Court of Iowa said in Blanchard v. Lambert, 43 Iowa 231, "in this state no express form is necessary, more than at common law, to constitute a valid marriage," citing Fenton v. Reed (Chancellor Kent's case). This statement was unnecessary as the case could have been and was disposed of on a number of other grounds. The marriage was a ceremonial one, the only question being the death or divorce of a former spouse of one of the parties.

In 1877 the Supreme Court of Missouri in the case of

Dyer v. Brannock, 66 Mo. 391-424, reviewed most all of the cases on the subject. In this case there was an agreement followed by immediate cohabitation. A child was born. The court held there was a valid marriage. The court does not say, however, what it would have done had there been no cohabitation but does say it must not be understood as giving an opinion in regard to a contract *per verba de futuro* followed by consummation.

In 1877, a case involving this subject came before the Supreme Court of Minnesota. (State v. Worthingham, 23 Minn. 528.) This was a proceedings in bastardy, instituted on the complaint of one Mary Sullivan which charged that she gave birth to a bastard child, of which defendant is alleged to be the father. The defendant resisted the proceedings on the ground that the child was legitimate by virtue of a valid common-law marriage between him and prosecuting witness. The parties lived together eight years and had five children born to them. The defendant had a wife living at the time he began living with prosecuting witness but procured a divorce from her two years later. It was held that there was a valid common-law marriage upon the removal of the impediment, the court saying:

> "An intercourse originally unlawful and lustful from choice undoubtedly raises the presumption that its character remains such during its continuance. But this is a presumption, not of law, but of fact, for the consideration of the jury in connection with the particular facts and circumstances of the case."

We have seen that in 1843 the doctrine was not so generally accepted as to be followed by the Supreme Court

of the United States. But from that time until the time
we are now considering, many states accepted the doctrine. So in the case of Meister v. Moore, 96 U. S. 826,
argued April 16, 1878, and decided April 29, 1878, the Supreme Court held that a contract of marriage *per verba
de præsenti is valid*. The opinion in the case is very brief.
The court says that it does not propose to examine in detail the numerous decisions that have been made by the
state courts. Speaking of marriages *per verba de præsenti, Mr. Justice Strong* says in that case:

> "That such a contract constitutes a marriage at
> common law there can be no doubt, in view of the
> adjudications made in this country, *from its earliest
> settlement to the present day*." (?)

The court says in reference to the Massachusetts doctrine:

> "So, in Massachusetts, it was early decided that
> a statute very like the Michigan statute rendered
> illegal a marriage which would have been good at
> common law, but which was not entered into in the
> manner directed by the written law. Milford v.
> Worcester, 7 Mass. 48. *It may well be doubted,
> however, whether such is now the law in that state.
> Parton v. Hervey, 1 Gray, 119, 1854.*

The last statement above quoted is difficult to explain.
Only four years before the decision in Meister v. Moore,
the Supreme Court of Massachusetts had approved of the
case of Milford v. Worcester. In Thompson v. Thompson, 114 Mass. 566, decided in 1874, the Massachusetts
court said:

> "To constitute a valid marriage by the law of the
> Commonwealth, it must be solemnized between par-
> ties competent to contract it, and (except in the
> case of Quakers) before a person being or profess-

ing to be a justice of the peace or minister of the gospel. *Milford v. Worcester, 7 Mass. 48* * * * The mere belief of either or both parties that they were husband and wife does not constitute a legal marriage.....A decree of nullity must, therefore, be entered as prayed for.''

The year following the decision in Meister v. Moore by the United States Supreme Court, the question was again presented to the Supreme Court of Massachusetts in the case of Commonwealth v. Munson, 127 Mass. 459. In that case Chief Justice Gray said:

"In Massachusetts, from very early times, the requisites of a valid marriage have been regulated by statute of the Colony, Province, and Commonwealth; the canon law was never adopted; and it was never received here as common law, that parties could by their own contract, without the presence of an officiating clergyman or magistrate, take each other as husband and wife, and so marry themselves. *Milford v. Worcester, 7 Mass. 48* * * * This clearly appears on tracing the history of the legislation upon the subject; the whole of which, whether repealed or unrepealed, is by a familiar rule to be considered in ascertaining the intention of the legislature * * * The decision on the second point in Parton v. Hervey, 1 Gray 119, was in exact accordance with the statement of Chief Justice Parsons in Milford v. Worcester * * The general statement of Mr. Justice Bigelow in the course of his discussion of this point—that, 'in the absence of any provision declaring marriages, not celebrated in the prescribed manner, or between parties of certain ages, absolutely void, it is held that all marriages regularly made according to the common law, are valid and binding, although had in violation of the specific regulations imposed by statute'' —evidently had regard to the fact of specific regulations as to the publication of banns or the consent of parents, and not to the broader question, which was not before him, whether any presence of a third person was necessary. *If the learned judge had intended to cast any doubt on the adjudication of that question in Milford v. Worcester, he hardly would have referred, as he did, to that case as supporting his statement.*"

The error of Justice Strong no doubt made it necessary for the Massachusetts court to controvert his statement which may be attributed to his lack of investigation.

Again, the Supreme Court says in Meister v. Moore, supra:

"As before remarked, the statutes are held merely directory; because marriage is a thing of common right; because it is the policy of the state to encourage it, [*does any state encourage marriages of this sort?*] and because, as has sometimes been said, any other construction would compel holding illegitimate the offspring of many parents *conscious of no violation of law.*" (Italics and insert mine.)

While the purpose of this work is to show only the development of common law marriages in the United States, yet the last statement should not be allowed to go unchallenged. During the recent war the Bureau of War Risk Insurance had before it, perhaps, more cases of alleged common law marriage than are contained in all of the reports of adjudicated cases put together. It must be remembered that there were upwards of four millions of men in the military and naval service. The men were compelled to make allotments from their pay to their wives and children unless good cause was shown for exemption. The Exemption Section of the Bureau of War Risk Insurance considered more than one hundred thousand claims for exemption from compulsory allotment, almost ten thousand of which were cases of married men who entered the service as single. Women claiming to be wives would file claim for family allowance and an investigation would be instituted. The writer had charge of these cases for a time and is in a position to say that by far the greater number of alleged marriages were meretricious relationships, for the convenience of the parties alone, and in a large percentage of the cases the reason no formal celebration of marriage was had was because one or the other, and in many cases both, of the parties were already married but separated from a former spouse. There was nearly always a ghost in the closet. Moreover, very few, if any, of these persons really believe that they are married. Scarcely any of these persons believe that a divorce is necessary to dissolve the marriage; in fact, nearly all believe that common-law marriage and living in adultery are synonomous terms. If it were a *sine qua non* to the validity of such a union that the parties believe that a divorce is necessary to dissolve such a marriage (and a divorce is necessary as in any other marriage), then there are few if any common law marriages. As is elsewhere shown, however, the parties may doubt the validity of the marriage and need not consider themselves married "in the eyes of the law"! Few of such persons believe that children of these unions are legitimate. But, says the Supreme Court, a strong reason for upholding such marriages is to legitimate the offspring of many parents conscious of no violation of law. The first part of this statement expresses a noble sentiment but the latter part borders on the ridiculous. *"Many* parents conscious of no violation of law," is a phrase which does not sound very well to one who has had actual experience in the handling of many of these cases. Again considering the first part of the statement, if these unions must be held valid marriages in order to render legitimate the unfortunate children thereof, the children of subsequent formal marriages of the parties must be bastardized. The great majority of common law marriages, so called, are not permanent unions. After a while the parties tire of each other and "marry" some one else and have children.

The following typical statement taken from one of the affidavits filed in the Bureau of War Risk Insurance by an alleged "common law wife" is interesting:

> "For a better understanding of my relationship to the deceased insured I wish to state that twenty-five years ago I was living as the common law wife of . . . . from which union I received two children. * * * After living with this man for about three and one-half years I *married* one . . . . , and this is the reason why I bear the name of . . . . * * * * I was never *married* to . . . . [the alleged common law husband] and my two children which I received through my union with him were never legitimate."

That this is the popular notion of the term is evidenced by the following Associated Press Dispatch which is taken from the Washington, D. C., Star of July 6, 1922:

> "Huntingdon, Pa., July 6.—Dr. Herbert Bryson, shell-shocked war veteran of Washington, D. C., lost his fight for temporary freedom here yesterday when after a habeas corpus hearing before Judge Thomas F. Bailey he was remanded to jail until he should face the court in September on a charge of the murder of his *common law wife*, Mrs. Helen Irene Haines, who was shot on April 8. Mrs.

Haines was the wife of a chauffeur of Washington. She disappeared with Dr. Bryson in the summer of 1921.''

It is interesting to observe the entirely different view taken by the Supreme Court of Maryland in Dennison v. Dennison, 35 Md. 380:

"These loose and irregular contracts as a general thing, derive no support from morals or religion, but are most generally founded in a wanton and licentious cohabitation. Hence the law of the state has given them no sanction.''

And the Supreme Court of New York in discussing the term "common-law wife," which is generally applied (although incorrect) by lawyers as well as laymen to the wife of a man by a common-law marriage, says:

"The term 'common law wife' is one not known to the law, and the law looks with no favor upon the connection indicated by it. As *properly* used this term is a synonym for a woman who, having lived in a state of concubinage with a man during the time when she might have been openly declared to be his wife if she were such, only seeks to assume that relation openly after his death, and when she is impelled to it by the loss of the support he had given her, and by a desire to obtain that support by sharing in the proceeds of his property." *In re* Brush, 49 N. Y. Supp. 803, 806, 25 App. Div. 610.[13]

---

[13]The fact is that a wife by a common law marriage is in contemplation of law no different than a wife by a ceremonial marriage. Some courts, however, refer to a widow of a man to whom she was not formally married as ''common law widow'' (Hulett v. Carey, 66 Minn. 327).

CHAPTER VIII

We have traced the development of informal marriages in the several states up to the time the common law doctrine was finally accepted' by the Supreme Court of the United States. The cases show that cohabitation was present in nearly every case considered. What would have been the decision had cohabitation not been present, we can only guess. The opinion of the writer is the doctrine never would have been accepted. In some states we have seen the earlier *dicta* overruled by subsequent decisions.

The common law rule of marriage *per verba de futuro cum copula* is not law in any American state today, yet the cases are full of dicta to the effect that they are valid. Where actual cases have arisen the doctrine has been repudiated, though not on the right ground.

By the *theory* of our law, independent of statute, marriage is very easily constituted. All that is required is the agreement. While there should be an intent to change the *status personarum*,[1] it is not necessary that the parties believe themselves ''married in the eyes of the law.''[2]

---

[1]McInnes v. More, H. of L. Cases, 1782.

[2]Tartt v. Negus, 127 Ala. 301, 28 So. 713. Through the courtesy of Mr. N. C. Calogeras of Denver, I have just been supplied with a copy of the decision of the Supreme Court of Colorado in the case of Cordas v. Ryan, decided July 3, 1922. The County Court held there was no common-law marriage. The District Court held there was. The Supreme Court of Colorado upheld the decision of the County Court. The facts in the case as found by the court are as follows: In 1919 and 1920 Frances Ryan, the

The Supreme Court of Alabama went to this extreme in the case of Tartt v. Negus, decided in 1899 wherein it is stated:

"The common law mode of marriage is recognized as valid in this State, and to constitute such

contestant, was working for Danicks as cashier and bookkeeper of his restaurant in Denver. He treated her affectionately and there is evidence that they had illicit relations. In 1919 and 1920 while she was in Kansas City, he wrote her letters; except one, however, these letters contain little if anything showing an engagement to marry; in that one he expresses the hope that she will be his wife. He wrote at least one letter to a friend saying he was going to marry her. In his will, dated January 6th, 1921, he left a legacy of $2,000 "to Frances Ryan, a faithful servant in my employment." On January 25th, 1921, being in very bad health, he went from Denver to French Lick Springs, Indiana, and took the contestant with him. They occupied the same stateroom and berth and she referred to him in his presence as her husband. They registered at the hotel at their destination as man and wife and treated each other as such. Getting no benefit at the Springs, he went to Rochester, Minnesota. There they registered and conducted themselves as before. He was treated in a hospital there and introduced her as his wife to doctors and nurses. During this journey she wrote a number of letters to friends and acquaintances of herself and testator, some purporting to be from them both, some signed by her in both names but her signatures were all "Frances" with no surname. She received letters under the name of Miss Frances Ryan. She did not indicate or suggest in her letters that she should be addressed otherwise nor that she was married nor did he in his letters. He underwent a severe surgical operation and died March 22nd, 1921. The body was brought to Denver for burial and the permission for removal required under the laws of Minnesota stated that it was to be "accompanied by Mrs. ? Nicholas Danicks as escort." She went to the funeral and testified that she there claimed to be "his nearest relative," (she does not say widow) and for that reason insisted on riding and did ride in a car nearer the hearse than the one to which she was first assigned. The funeral was on Sunday. On Monday she consulted a lawyer and on Wednesday she was advised that her marriage revoked the will and proceeded accordingly. The court said: "The court below also put its decision partly on the ground that relations will be presumed to be moral rather than immoral. Some cases so state and the principals may be a true one, but to rest a case of proof of marriage on that alone is to presume every sexual relation moral. The proof by conduct alone of a common law contract of marriage must have at least something in it not merely consistent with marriage but inconsistent with any other relation. There is not here that 'habit and repute of marriage' which is often such strong evidence of an actual matrimonial contract."

marriage it is only necessary that there shall exist a mutual consent or agreement between the parties to be husband and wife, following by cohabitation and living together as husband and wife. If such was the status of Gus and Polly Mescepts, *the law established the relation of marriage without regard to what the parties considered the legal effect to be.* It was, therefore, not essential to the validity of the marriage that Gus Mescepts should have considered Polly to be his wife, as is in effect asserted by plaintiffs' requested charges 6, 8 and 9; *nor was it necessary to the marriage that the agreement should have been in terms 'to be husband and wife in the eyes of the law,'* as stated in charge 12."

They may even doubt the validity of their marriage. Lord Stowell said in the Dalrymple case:

"But supposing that Miss Gordon really did entertain doubts with respect to the validity of her marriage, what could be the effect of such doubts? Surely not to annul the marriage, if it were otherwise unimpeached. We are, at this moment, inquiring with all the assistance of all the learned professors of law in that country, amongst whom there is great discordance of opinion, what is the effect of such contracts. That private persons, compelled to the necessity of a secret marriage, might entertain doubts whether they had satisfied the demands of a law which has been rendered so doubtful, will not affect the real sufficiency of the measures they had taken.'"[3]

In this connection is the following from the case of Van Tuyl v. Van Tuyl, decided by the Supreme Court of New York in 1869 (57 Barb. 235):

"It is urged, however, that it being a part of the agreement proved in this case, that the marriage should at some time thereafter be solemnized in church, the same was void, because the contract, *per*

---

[3]Dalrymple v. Dalrymple, 2 Hagg. Const. 76.

verba de præsenti, constitutes marriage only when the parties intend that it shall do so without any subsequent ceremony. This rule of law is probably correct, for the reason stated by Lord Campbell in the Queen v. Willis, (10 Cl. & F. 534,) that 'it is easy to conceive that parties might contract *per verba de præsenti* without meaning instantly to become man and wife.' "

The foregoing statement needs explanation. The true rule is stated by Mr. Bishop as follows:

"As in consent *per verba de præsenti,* so in *per verba de futuro cum copula,* if something—as, for example, a formal solemnization—is by the understanding of both the parties to take place before they shall become husband and wife, marriage is not constituted. Copula does not make them married. But this doctrine should not be misunderstood. Mere secrecy, and a mere intent to have a future solemnization, will not alone prevent the transaction from becoming matrimony." (Marr. Div. & Sep. Book 1, Sect. 364).

Secret Marriages

The question whether or not an agreement to keep an informal marriage secret invalidates it, is also a subject in regard to which there is lack of uniformity in the decisions of the courts of this country, due to the fact that the subject has not been given thorough consideration.

While in theory under the canon law an absolutely secret marriage could be contracted, yet for practical purposes it was dissoluble at will as the canon law required in general two witnesses. Thus, the maxim of the canon law is *clandestinium manifesto non præiudicat.* But the later English cases seem not to have followed this rule.

In the case of Dalrymple v. Dalrymple (2 Hagg. Consist. 54) Lord Stowell said:

> "An engagement of secrecy is perfectly consistent with the most valid, and even with the most regular marriages. It frequently exists even in them from prudential reasons; from the same motives it almost always does in private or clandestine marriages. It is only an evidence against the existence of a marriage, when no such prudential reasons can be assigned for it, and where everything, arising from the very nature of marriage, calls for its publication."

In 1884 the Supreme Court of the United States held, in the case of the State of Maryland for the use of Markley v. Baldwin (112 U. S. 490), that some public recognition is necessary to the validity of an informal marriage. Mr. Justice Field said:

> "Upon the issue made by the first plea, evidence was introduced to establish a marriage between Markley's mother and the deceased. It showed that her maiden name was Rebecca Markley; that, whilst retaining that name, she lived with him, he passing also by the name of Markley; that they had several children; that to her sisters and to one Cross, his son-in-law, he frequently spoke of her as his wife; that he so called her in their presence, and she called him her husband, and to the doctor who attended her during her confinement he spoke of her as his wife. *No witness was present at any marriage ceremony or at any contract of marriage between the parties; a marriage was inferred from their declarations and their living together.* * * * * *
>
> "As the case must, for this error, go back for a new trial, it is proper to say that, by the law of Pennsylvania, where, if at all, the parties were married, a marriage is a civil contract, and may be made *per verba de præsenti*, that is, by words in the present tense, without attending ceremonies, re-

ligious or civil. Such also is the law of many other States in the absence of statutory regulation. It is the doctrine of the common law. But, where no such ceremonies are required and no record is made to attest the marriage, some public recognition of it is necessary as evidence of its existence. The protection of the parties and their children and considerations of public policy require this public recognition; and it may be made in any way which can be seen and known by men, such as living together as man and wife, treating each other and speaking of each other in the presence of third parties as being in that relation, and declaring the relation in documents executed by them whilst living together, such as deeds, wills and other formal instruments. From such recognition the reputation of being married will obtain among friends, associates and acquaintances, which is of itself evidence of a persuasive character. Without it the existence of the marriage will always be a matter of uncertainty; and the charge of the court should direct the jury to its necessity in the absence of statutory regulations on the subject. Otherwise the jury would be without any guide in their deliberations.''

''The law of Pennsylvania, as we are advised, requires, in some form, such recognition. See Nathan's Case, 2 Brew. 149, 153; Commonwealth v. Stump, 53 Pa. St. 132.''

The question in this case seems to be not whether a marriage *per verba de præsenti* was contracted, but whether a marriage may be inferred from habit and repute which, as we have elsewhere seen, is not common law marriage at all.

The second paragraph of the statement of the Supreme Court above quoted is, in the opinion of the present writer, doubtful in so far as some public recognition of a common-law marriage is necessary to its validity. It may also be argued that the Supreme Court intended merely to state the law of Pennsylvania on this question, and did so incorrectly. However, it is not entirely clear that Justice Field meant to limit his language to the law of Pennsylvania.

On the other hand, it must be admitted that the statement is not absolutely necessary to the decision in the case which involves not the validity of a common law marriage, but the question whether the marriage might be presumed from habit and repute. The Supreme Court of California in the case of Sharon v. Sharon (75 Calif. 1) decided in 1888, refused to follow this decision of the Supreme Court. In the Sharon case the court said:

> "While this action was pending in the court below, a judgment of the circuit court of the United States for Maryland was reversed by the supreme court of the United States. (State of Maryland for the Use of Markley v. Baldwin, 112 U. S. 490.) One of the issues there was, Was Markley, the real plaintiff, a son and heir of Daniel Lord, deceased? And it involved the validity of an alleged marriage between the deceased and the mother of the plaintiff. In the circuit court there was a general verdict for the defendants.
>
> "Mr. Justice Field said that, as for the error mentioned the cause must go back for a new trial, it was proper to say that by the law of Pennsylvania, where, if at all, the parties were married, a marriage could be made *per verba de præsenti,* without attending ceremonies, religious or civil; that such is the doctrine of the common law. 'But where no such ceremonies are required, and no record is made to attest the marriage, some public recognition of it is necessary as evidence of its existence.' He adds, the charge of the court should direct the jury as to the necessity of such recognition in the absence of statutory regulations on the subject. And the learned judge said: 'The law of Pennsylvania, as

8

we are advised, requires in some form such recognition. See Nathan's Case, 2 Brewst. 149, 153; Commonwealth v. Stump, 53 Pa. St. 132.'

"In Maryland v. Baldwin no witness was present at any marriage ceremony, or at any contract of marriage; a marriage, if it existed, was to be inferred from their declarations and living together (p. 493, 494). The language of the court is to be interpreted in view of the facts. If, however, as claimed by appellant, it was intended to be said that, when there is direct evidence of a contract of marriage, by words in the present tense, there must also, by the law of Pennsylvania, be evidence of a public recognition of the marriage, a reference to the two cases cited shows that the learned judge was wrongly advised as to the law of that state.

"In Commonwealth v. Stump the supreme court of Pennsylvania decided: 'Where there is no proof of actual marriage, cohabitation and reputation are necessary to ground a presumption of marriage; proof of cohabitation alone is insufficient.' (Commonwealth v. Stump, 53 Pa. St. 132, 135; 91 Am. Dec. 198.)

"In Nathan's Case the court of quarter sessions held that the wife was a competent witness to prove a present contract to marry; and independent of her testimony (p. 168), the marriage was sufficiently proved by the acts and declarations of the parties; that reputation and cohabitation are sufficient evidence of marriage, and may be conclusive where the rights of third persons are affected, and the legitimacy of children called in question. * * *.''

In Volume II, Schouler on Marriage, Divorce, Separation and Domestic Relations (published in 1921) there is a separate section entitled ''SECRET MARRIAGES'' which reads: ''There is a presumption against the validity of secret marriages.'' The case cited in support of the statement seems to bear out the text. It is the case of Sorenson v. Sorenson, decided by the Supreme Court of

Nebraska in 1903 (68 Neb. 483). The court cites with approval the decision of the Supreme Court of the United States in Maryland v. Baldwin, supra. Three rehearings were granted in the Sorenson case. On the second rehearing the court examined the evidence and held it was not sufficient to establish a common law marriage. The court said:

> "There was a time, perhaps, when the doctrine of a liberal construction of the testimony and slight proof of a common-law marriage subserved a useful purpose; but if it ever did, that time is long since past. There is nothing to be said in its favor now. Especially is this so in this state, where the legislature has undertaken to provide for the formal solemnization of the marriage rites, if not in public, at least in the presence of witnesses, and have the fact of the marriage preserved in records provided for that purpose by the state. This ancient doctrine is alien to the ideas and customs of our people. It tends to weaken the public estimate of the sanctity of the marriage relation. It puts in doubt the certainty of the rights of inheritance. It opens the door to false pretenses of marriage and the imposition upon estates of supposititious heirs. It places honest, God-ordained matrimony and mere meretricious cohabitation too nearly on a level with each other. In view of these consequences, that are apparent to all, it seems to us that grave consideration of public policy require us to closely scrutinize the testimony offered and the proof adduced in support of every common-law marriage, alleged to have been consummated in this state."

On the third rehearing the court said:

> "After his death she sought to establish an interest in his property on the ground that they were engaged to be married; she spoke of this to several persons, and did not claim that she was his wife, but alleged that he had agreed to marry her. If

she knew herself to be his lawful wife, and had consented to keep it secret until a public ceremony
could be performed, it is difficult to understand why,
when death had prevented the public ceremony, she
should fail *to at once declare the truth*. She did not
assert that she had ever been his wife until after
several attempts to obtain his property had failed,
and she had learned that only as his widow could
such an attempt succeed. Further details of the
facts disclosed by this record may be found in the
former opinions.

"Our marriage laws aim at publicity. To allege
that these laws have been disregarded, and that a
secret marriage has been entered into, is to cast
suspicion upon the conduct of the parties. Subsequent cohabitation, and holding each other out to
the world as husband and wife furnish strong cor-
roboration of the existence of the contract. *Where
these elements of proof are wanting, and, one party
being deceased, the existence of the contract rests
wholly upon the unsupported testimony of the other
party, the presumption raised by the circumstances
amounts to proof opposed to the marriage contract
itself.* We do not think that the evidence of this
witness is so direct, certain and consistent as to establish the contract of marriage in the face of this
presumption."

The following statement by McFarland, one of the three
dissenting Justices in the case of Sharon v. Sharon, supra,
is worthy of mention:

"But, as counsel have discussed with great learning and ability the requisites of a valid common-law
marriage, we may say, in passing by the subject,
that it is by no means clear that at any time in England a present contract followed by nothing more
than secret sexual intercourse constituted a perfect
marriage at common law. There are innumerable
authorities upon the subject, and they greatly conflict. In some cases the law is strained in favor of
the legitimacy of children, and of persons criminally

charged. But in cases like the one at bar, of direct attempts to establish marriage, the weight of authorities seem to be against the positions taken by respondent. * * *''

The following, also from the dissenting opinion above referred to, is, in the opinion of the present writer, entirely correct:

"And it is rare, indeed, to find a case at common law where *any* respectable court has held a marriage entirely secret to be valid. In the Queen v. Millis, the attorney-general and the solicitor general were contending for the validity of the marriage there in question, where the ceremony was performed by a Presbyterian preacher, and not by a minister of the established church; and in nearly every authority cited by them there had been an agreement of marriage before witnesses, and generally some form of religious ceremony. And it must be remembered that the 'clandestine marriage' referred to in the authorities was by no means a secret marriage; it was a marriage entered into before witnesses, usually with an irregular ceremony,—without the publication of banns, and lacking other requisites of the ecclesiastical law. Even the Fleet and Gretna Green marriages were not secret. * * *''3a

From every point of view there is much to be said in favor of the statement of Justice Field, above quoted. Although the case has been approved quite frequently by the courts, it is scarcely ever referred to by a writer on Marriage or Domestic Relations.

3aThere are various degrees of clandestinity: (1). Marriages absolutely secret and, by the canon law unprovable because of the rule *Clandestinium Manifesto non præindicat.* 2). Marriages not solemnized *in facie ecclesiæ.* (3). Marriages not preceded by publication of banns. Esmein Le Marriage En Droit Canonique I, 181, 182. Pollock and Maitland say the Council of Trent very wisely required the testimony of the parish priest. Bk. II, p. 374.

NECESSITY OF COHABITATION

The books are full of cases in which the statement is made that a valid common-law marriage may be created in this country by an agreement without consummation or cohabitation.   An examination of the cases generally shows, however, that the statement is not necessary to the decision in the case as the parties actually consummated the marriage or lived together in the relation of husband and wife.

The true condition of the cases on the subject has been clearly set forth by Prof. Long, in his treatise on Domestic Relations. He says:

> "As to whether mere consent without cohabitation is sufficient in American law to constitute a valid common-law marriage, where common-law marriages are recognized as valid, is not settled. As might be expected, there are practically no actual decisions on the question. *Cases of bona fide informal marriages not followed by consummation or cohabitation must be among the rarest of human transactions.* And practically all the cases which have been found in which the validity of informal marriages has been considered, are cases in which the parties had cohabited or at least had sexual relations.   In all such cases any declarations by the courts as to the necessity for consummation are, therefore, plainly by way of *dicta*."

This learned writer further states that while by the common law mere present consent without consummation seems to have constituted a valid marriage, and on strictly legal principles, mere consent without consummation should be held to constitute a valid common-law marriage, yet, however, the weight of judicial opinion is probably opposed to this doctrine.   (2nd Ed. Sect. 68.)

And to the same effect is the following from Volume 2, page 1435, of Schouler, Marriage, Divorce, Separation and Domestic Relations:

> "Section 1177. *Public Cohabitation Necessary.*
> "There is much conflict in the decisions whether public cohabitation is essential in this country for a common-law marriage, but it seems to be the general view that to constitute a marriage *per verba de præsenti* cohabitation subsequently is necessary, just the same as in case of a marriage *per verba de futuro.*
> "Marriage is more than a contract: it is a status created by mutual consent of one man and one woman. The only difference between a formal marriage under license and a common-law marriage is in the method of expressing consent. The cohabitation must be professedly as husband and wife, and public, so that by their conduct towards each other they may be known as husband and wife. *To allow a private agreement to operate as a common-law marriage would open the door to fraud of all kinds and make the estates of wealthy men the prey of the adventuress.*"

The learned author of the note in L. R. A. 1915 E has correctly observed the following:

> "There are decisions which squarely declare that consent must be followed by cohabitation; but it is found that, for the most part, the few cases in which the statements are not mere *obiter dicta,* or based on statutes, either dispose of the matter without discussion or are based on considerations inconsistent with the recognition of consensual marriage in any form, or decided largely in reliance upon decisions that cannot be regarded as authority on the point."

On the other hand it has also been correctly observed by the Supreme Court of Texas that:

"There are a number of cases in which the 'stock phrase'—'Marriage is a civil contract, and to constitute such marriage requires only the agreement of the man and the woman to become then and thenceforth husband and wife'—is used; but in each case which sustained the marriage, [except the two mentioned by the court], there was cohabitation." (Grigsby v. Rieb, 105 Texas 597; 153 S. W. 1124; L. R. A. 1915 E. 1.)

Thus in the oft referred to case of Hulett v. Carey, decided by the Supreme Court of Minnesota in 1896 (66 Minn. 327, 69 N. W. 31, 34 L. R. A. 384, 61 Am. St. 419), following the dictum of Lord Stowell in the Dalrymple case the court held that an agreement to keep the marriage secret does not invalidate it (but no mention was made of the decision of the Supreme Court of the United States) and also said *arguendo* that cohabitation is not necessary to the validity of a marriage if it is entered into *per verba de præsenti*. In this case the petitioner presented her petition for an allowance of homestead to her as Hulett's widow and for the vacation of the probate of his will on the ground that it had been revoked by his marriage to her subsequent to its execution. Hulett, generally supposed and reputed to be a bachelor, died July 25, 1892. The petitioner claimed to have become his wife by virtue of a written contract of marriage as follows:

"January 6, 1892. Contract of marriage between N. Hulett and Mrs. L. A. Pomeroy. Believing a marriage by contract to be perfectly lawful, we do hereby agree to be husband and wife, and to hereafter live together as such. In witness whereof we have hereunto set our hands the day and year first above written. (Signed) N. Hulett, L. A. Pomeroy."

The principal question before the court was whether there had been a valid marriage between the parties. The court by Justice Mitchell said:

"* * * The respondent has been for a long time prior to the execution of the marriage contract in the employment of Hulett as housekeeper at his farm at Stoney Point, some miles out of the city of Duluth. Her testimony is that immediately after the execution of this contract she moved into his room, and that from henceforth until his death they occupied the same sleeping apartment, and cohabitated together as husband and wife. But she admits that it was agreed between them that their marriage was to be kept secret until they could move into Duluth, and go to housekeeping in a house which Hulett owned in that city. While a feeble effort was made to prove that their marital relation had become known to one or two persons, yet we consider the evidence conclusive that their marriage contract was kept secret, that they never publicly assumed marital relations, or held themselves out to the public as husband and wife, but, on the contrary, so conducted themselves as to leave the public under the impression that their former relations of employer and housekeeper remained unchanged.

"Upon this state of facts the contention of the appellants is that there was no marriage, notwithstanding the execution by them of the written contract; that, in order to constitute a valid common-law marriage, the contract, although in *verba de præsenti*, must be followed by habit or reputation of marriage,—that is, as we understand counsel, by the public assumption of marital relations. We do not so understand the law. The law views marriage as being merely a civil contract, not differing from any other contract, except that it is not revocable or dissoluble at the will of the parties. The essence of the contract of marriage is the consent of the parties, as in the case of any other contract; and, whenever there is a present, perfect consent to be husband and wife, the contract of marriage is completed. The authorities are practically unanimous to this effect.

"Marriage is a civil contract *jure gentium*, to the validity of which the consent of parties able to contract is all that is required by natural or public law. If the contract is made *per verba de præsenti*, and remains without cohabitation, or if made *per verba de futuro,* and be followed by consummation, it amounts to a valid marriage in the absence of any civil regulations to the contrary. 2 Kent, Comm. p. 87; 2 Greenl. Ev. Sect. 460; 1 Bish. & Mar. Div. Sects. 218, 227-229. The maxim of the civil law was *'Consensus non concubitus facit matrimonium.'* The whole law on the subject is that to render competent parties husband and wife they must and need only agree in the present tense to be such, no time being contemplated to elapse before the assumption of the status. If cohabitation follows, it adds nothing in law, although it may be evidence of marriage. It is mutual, present consent, lawfully expressed, which makes the marriage. 1 Bish. Mar. Div. & Sep., Sects. 239, 313, 315, 317. See, also, the leading case of Dalrymple v. Dalrymple, 2 Hagg. Consist. 54, which is the foundation of much of the law on the subject.

"An agreement to keep the marriage secret does not invalidate it, although the fact of secrecy might be evidence that no marriage ever took place. Dalrymple v. Dalrymple, supra. The only two cases which we have found in which anything to the contrary was actually decided are Reg. v. Millis, 10 Clark & F. 534, and Jewell v. Jewell, 1 How. 219; the court in each case being equally divided. But these cases have never been recognized as the law, either in England or in this country.   *   *   *''

The contract of marriage in this case, it will be observed, was written, so many of the arguments usually advanced against secret unions are not applicable to this case. So much of the opinion as relates to the necessity of cohabitation was unnecessary as the parties actually

cohabited.   And we have elsewhere seen that the statement that Regina v. Millis was never recognized in England is incorrect.

In a Missouri case (Davis v. Stoffer, 132 Mo. App. 555)
it was also argued that cohabitation is unnecessary to the
validity of a common-law marriage although there was
cohabitation in the case and the discussion was really
obiter.   This case, too, has been cited with approval by
courts and text-writers very frequently.

The dicta in these two cases was sufficient, however, to
convince a United States district court that such was the
law of those states.   This decision and the cases given
below are practically the only cases where the doctrine
has been expressly upheld.   In two of these cases it will
also be observed that there was a ceremony but not a com-
pliance with the law.

In the case of Dumaresly v. Fishly, decided by the Supreme Court of Kentucky in 1821 (10 Ky. 368) the rule
per verba de præsenti without cohabitation was upheld.
A marriage license was obtained in Louisville, Kentucky,
and the parties went across the river to Jeffersonville, Indiana, where they were married by a Catholic priest.
They never cohabited after their marriage, and the alleged husband slandered the wife and she brought an action to which he pleaded that the action did not lie because
he was her lawful husband.   Upon this issue the Kentucky
court held in favor of the husband sustaining the marriage.   In this case the court said:

> "Marriage and cohabitation are two things.   The
> latter is the object to be obtained by the former,
> and, to make it lawful, must be preceded by the
> former.   It is said, indeed, that a marriage con-

tracted *per verba de futuro,* which is in truth nothing but a promise to marry in future, is a valid marriage if the parties afterwards cohabit; but the cohabitation, even in that case, does not constitute the marriage. It is only evidence of the marriage; and the same authorities which say that a contract *per verba de futuro* becomes a marriage if the parties afterwards cohabit, invariably lay down the doctrine that a marriage *per verba præsenti* is, forthwith, a marriage, and complete without cohabitation.''

The facts in the case of Jackson v. Winne, decided by the Supreme Court of New York in 1828 (7 Wend. 47, 22 Am. Dec. 563) have been well stated by the Supreme Court of Texas as follows:

''It appeared that Enoch was arrested in the year 1800 on the complaint of the overseers of the poor of the town of Blenheim, under the bastardy act, on a charge of having gotten Joanna with child. He was taken to the house of Joanna's father, and thence with the father and the mother of Joanna, in company of the constable, to a justice of the peace to be married. The justice asked Enoch and Joanna if they consented to be married, and told them to join hands. Enoch dropped his hand and turned from Joanna. She took it and held it until they were pronounced man and wife. The justice hesitated when Enoch refused to take Joanna's hand, but proceeded in a minute or two and concluded the ceremony. It was customary for the justice to offer a prayer; but he did not do so on this occasion, and Joanna's father did so instead. During the whole time, Enoch said nothing. After the ceremony, Joanna returned to her father's house, but Enoch did not go with her; nor did they ever afterwards cohabit. Under that state of facts, the court held that the marriage was valid. There was neither cohabitation nor contract; but that court held that it was a contract on the part of the man, who being a prisoner, stood mute, refusing his hand to the woman,

who seized it and made the declarations. If it be
conceded that Enoch by silence gave consent, and
thereby made a contract, then to become and thereafter to be her husband, it stands as one of two
cases within my reach that sustain the proposition
that a marriage by contract alone establishes the
status of husband and wife.''

In the case of United States v. Simpson decided by the
Supreme Court of the Territory of Utah in 1885, it was
held that the mutual consent to a present marriage by
parties capable of contracting, though not followed by cohabitation, is a valid marriage. The court said:

"No form or ceremony is required, and no record
of marriage is kept. Marriage is left as it was at
common-law, and a consensual marriage is in all
respects valid. There need be no witnesses present.
If the parties are competent to contract, all that is
essential is a present agreement. The marriage is
complete when there is a full, free and mutual consent by the parties capable of contracting, though
not followed by cohabitation: Caryolle v. Ferrie,
26 Barb. 177; Bunting v. Leppingwell, 6 Coke Rep.
29; Jesson v. Collins, 6 Mod. 155; Fenton v. Reed,
4 John. 52; Jackson v. Winne, 7 Wend. 47; Hutchins v. Kimmel, 31 Mich. 130; Graham v. Bennett,
2 Cal. 503; Case v. Case, 17 Cal. 598; Rose v. Clark,
8 Paige, 574; Com. v. Stump, 53 Pa. St. 132.
Cohabitation is but one of the many incidents to
the marriage relation. It is not essential to it:
Murphy v. Ramsey, 114 U. S. 42.
Under our law a marriage depends solely upon
the mutual consent of the contracting parties. They
may enter into the marriage relation secretly, and
the fact may be unknown to all save the man and
woman.
As was said on the argument, a couple may meet
on the highway at any time in the day or night and
there contract a valid marriage. Whether it tends
to good morals to leave the matter thus loose, and

completely at the will of the parties it is not for us to discuss. That is a matter for the legislature. We have to take the law as we find it.'' (4 Utah 227.)

The Federal case already referred to is the case of Great Northern Railway v. Johnson (254 Fed. 683) decided in 1918. In this case the plaintiff brought suit to recover damages for the death of her alleged husband, and claimed to be his wife through a common-law marriage. The deceased signed a contract of marriage in duplicate where he resided in Minnesota, and sent both copies to plaintiff, who executed both copies in Missouri. One copy she retained and the other she returned to deceased. There is nothing to show that they ever thereafter lived together. The contract reads as follows:

> St. Paul, Minnesota,
> March 10, 1916.
> ''It is hereby agreed, by and between E. R. Spiers and Mayme Woodall, from this date henceforth to be husband and wife, and from this date henceforth to conduct ourselves toward each other as husband and wife, the said E. R. Spiers to contribute to the support and maintenance of said Mayme Woodall as her husband, and the said Mayme Woodall to conduct herself toward the said E. R. Spiers as a dutiful wife.''
> (Signed) E. R. Spiers
> Mayme Woodall.

The court said:

> ''The State of Minnesota recognizes common-law marriages, but the contract is governed by the laws of the State of Missouri, where acceptance by plaintiff of the contractual offer made by deceased occurred. That state recognizes and enforces common law marriages. * * * Under these decisions the rule seems to be that marriage is a civil contract,

possessing in its creation in *præsenti* the elements, and only the elements attaching to any contract, but that because it establishes a legal status of grave concern to the state and society, and because of the natural temptations to perjury, and the difficulties of combating such testimony, both of which frequently arise, the courts will closely scrutinize testimony intended to establish such a contract after the death of one of the parties thereto.

"In approaching the proposition that the parties must be together or within the same jurisdiction, it is to be noted that this matter of marriage is for the states, except in the District of Columbia and the Territories, and is to be determined by the law of the state where it was contracted or celebrated. So far as the law on the point here involved has been defined by the adjudications of the Missouri courts, it will be followed, irrespective of the view which might be taken by this court, if the question were open. A careful examination of the above cited Missouri cases and the many others from that state, convinces that in that state the marriage contract possesses the elements of an ordinary contract and none others. That contract establishes a very important status, but the contract itself is no respect peculiar. Mutual assent to the present institution of the status is all sufficient. No other act, such as cohabitation (Davis v. Stouffer, 132 Mo. App. 555; 112 S. W. 262), is necessary to complete the institution of the status where the mutual assent contemplates a marriage in *præsenti*. Why should the physical presence of the parties be essential to the legality of this contract, any more than of any other? It is not for us to devise means of making common law marriage difficult. It is our duty to recognize the law as it exists. Nor is there any reason why the parties should be within the same jurisdiction. The existence and validity of the contract must be determined by the law of the place where it is legally regarded as made. Here, however, there is no point in the suggestion, for both

of the states involved approve common law marriages.'' Judgment for plaintiff affirmed.

The cases in which it has been expressly held that cohabitation is essential to the validity of an informal marriage are fewer in number than one might suppose.
While there are a great number of cases in which the
court says cohabitation is essential, it will nearly always
be observed that the facts in the case showed cohabitation
and the statement that cohabitation is necessary is really
obiter dictum. For a case to be considered as ruling on
this question it would seem that there should be present
no cohabitation. Referring to the many statements found
in the reports that cohabitation is not necessary to the
validity of an informal marriage the Supreme Court of
Texas says that for a decision to be authority for the
proposition that a marriage is complete by the contract
without cohabitation, the case must not embrace in its facts
cohabitation or any form of consummation, for it would
not then be a case of marriage by contract only; and if
the case does involve cohabitation, any statement that cohabitation is unnecessary is a dictum. (Grigsby v. Rieb,
105 Tex. 597.) This argument is equally applicable to the
case where there is cohabitation and cohabitation is held
to be a requisite, a fact which the Texas court itself overlooked. There are a few cases, however, which do expressly hold that cohabitation is essential. Thus is the
case of Lorimer v. Lorimer, decided by the Supreme
Court of Michigan in 1900 (124 Mich. 631) the court said:

> ''It is claimed that the judge did not properly in-
> struct the jury in relation to what was sufficient to
> constitute a valid marriage. He used the following
> language in his charge to the jury:

" 'This plaintiff comes before you, in court, claiming to be the lawful wife of the late Thomas Lorimer. On her is the burden of proof of showing that she is the lawful wife, there being no marriage certificate and no marriage ceremony. On her is the burden of showing that her mind and the mind of Thomas Lorimer once met,—met at the time that she said that they agreed to take each other for husband and wife, and to live in relations as such; that they made a bargain about it. And, in stating that, I say, if they did in their minds fully meet,—if they did come to a full understanding,—and you should find that, then, under the law of this State, they were married. That is the whole test of the matter.'

> "We think this charge was too restricted, and that it was not cured by any other portion of the charge. Our courts have gone a good way to sustain the validity of a marriage where an agreement to live and cohabit together as husband and wife has been made and acted upon. But at no time has it been said that, in the absence of a valid marriage ceremony, a simple agreement to live together, even though the parties intended to carry out the agreement, is sufficient to constitute a valid marriage, unless acted upon by living together and cohabiting as husband and wife."

It is a mistake of principle to require, in addition to consent, evidence of cohabitation as essential to the validity of an informal marriage. The only function of evidence of cohabitation is to show consent. Copula is not necessary to the validity of a formal marriage and on principle it should not be necessary in the case of an informal marriage. On this point the Supreme Court of Massachusetts has said:

> "The consummation of a marriage by coition is not necessary to its validity. The status of the parties is fixed in law when the marriage contract is

9

entered into in the manner prescribed by the stat-
utes in relation to the solemnization of marriages.
Eaton v. Eaton, 122 Mass. 276; Dies v. Winne, 7
Wend. (N. Y.) 47; Dumaresly v. Fishly, 3 A. K.
Marsh (Ky.) 368; Patrick v. Patrick, 3 Phillim.
Ecc. 496; Dalrymple v. Dalrymple, 2 Hagg. Const.
54.'' (Franklin v. Franklin, 154 Mass. 515, 28 N.
E. 681, 13 L. R. A. 843, 26 Am. St. 266, 1891.)

The copula does not constitute marriage, but is taken,
when circumstances justify it, as evidence of the performance of the previous promise. The Supreme Court of
Missouri correctly observed that establishing a marriage
is a very different thing from the marriage itself. And in
the same case (Davis v. Stouffer, 132 Mo. App. 566) the
court said:

> ''No one could say that reputation of marriage
> was any part of the marriage for the simple reason
> that there could not be a rightful reputation of mar-
> riage until after the marriage; and so cohabitation
> is not a part of the marriage, for it can only law-
> fully exist *after* the marriage.''

If only copula were required in addition to consent we
would be recognizing the ancient doctrine maintained by
Gratian and other canonists in force prior to the Lombardian distinctions and this would be difficult to defend
on principle. The dicta of the cases go much farther,
however. The cases purport to require cohabitation,
which presupposes not one but perhaps many acts of
copulation. A doctrine that requires two persons to for-
nicate a number of times before they create a legal status
is absurd. Must they live together as husband and wife
before they are husband and wife and this too in the face
of a provision of the criminal law that persons who do

this without first being married are guilty of a crime? Again, just where will the line be drawn? When do the parties cease to be fornicators and just when does the sublime institution of matrimony begin? The Supreme Court of California has wisely observed that "it is incredible the legislature intended that copulation may take place before the marriage is complete, or to put it in the power of the man after he has enjoyed the person of the woman to say 'I will proceed no further.'" (Sharon v. Sharon, 79 Cal. 700.) If the idea of an informal marriage without cohabitation is undesirable doctrine, the remedy lies not in requiring cohabitation, but as a careful writer observes "in the entire abrogation of the common law, a course that, in the present age has something to commend it." (L. R. A. 1915 E note.) We are in entire accord with the following conclusion of this same writer:

> "If a mutual agreement in fact is clearly established by direct evidence, neither holding out nor cohabitation is necessary to constitute the parties husband and wife. While these circumstances are of considerable probative force in establishing consent, they are not its essential concomitants. This was a principle of the common law, which was accepted in Scotland and supposedly in England. A contract *per verba de præsenti* was regarded as *ipsum matrimonium*. This view is the proper one, for since by 'cohabitation' is meant not merely sexual intercourse, but openly living together as husband and wife, as is commonly held, and since this entails the lapse of time sufficient to enable the public to judge the relations of the parties, the result would be in most instances of marriage by private consent, that there would be sexual intercourse before the completion of the marriage by 'cohabitation as husband and wife,' a result exactly contrary to the real purpose of marriage laws."

There is absolutely no authority in any of the English cases to support the theory that cohabitation is essential to an informal marriage. The following statements have been selected from two of the leading English cases on the subject.

In the case of Lindo v. Belisario decided in 1795 (1 Hagg. Cons. Rep. 216) Lord Stowell said:

> "The rule prevailed in all times, as the rule of the canon law, which existed in this country and in Scotland, till other civil regulations interfered in this country; and it is the rule which prevails in many countries of the world, at this day, that a mutual engagement, or betrothment, is a good marriage, without consummation, according to the law of nature, and binds the parties accordingly, as the terms of other contracts would do, respecting the engagements which they purport to describe. If they agree, and pledge their troth to resign to each other the use of their persons, for the purpose of raising a common offspring, by the law of nature that is complete. It is not necessary that actual use and possession should have intervened to complete the *vinculum fidei*. The *vinculum* follows on the contract, without consummation, if expressed in present terms; and the canon law itself, with all its attachments to ecclesiastical forms, adopts this view of the subject, as is well described by Swinburne in his book on Espousals, where he says 'that it is a present and perfect consent, the which alone maketh matrimony, without either public solemnization or carnal copulation, for neither is the one, nor the other, the essence of matrimony, but consent only.' "

Concerning the necessity of cohabitation to effect a marriage where consent is exchanged *per verba de præsenti,* the Lord President said in the case of Yelverton v. Longworth (4 Macq. H. L. C. 803):

"The consent which is to constitute marriage must be mutual consent of parties, unequivocally and seriously expressed, with the view and for the purpose of constituting the married relation—interchange of consent *de præsenti,* to be as from that date husband and wife—constituting as from that moment, by that interchange of consent, the relation of husband and wife. It is not necessary towards the constitution of marriage in that way that it shall have been followed by cohabitation. Such I hold to be the established law of this country."

As has already been stated, the difficulty a number of American courts have found with this question arises out of the fact that they confuse what is necessary to *create* an informal marriage with what is necessary to *prove* the marriage. In one very recent case the court goes so far as to say "it is apparent that, though sometimes ignored, it is necessary that an assumption of marriage relations be had to constitute a common-law marriage." (In re Peterson's Estate, 22 N. D. 480, 1912.) The authorities cited by the court relate only to the question of *proof* of marriage.

There are as we have seen but few cases in the reports where marriages *per verba de præsenti* without cohabitation have been sustained. A number of cases arose during the war, however, where girls living in states ostensibly recognizing the rule, wished to marry American soldiers in France. Largely because of dicta in the cases, many of these marriages were held valid for War Risk Insurance and other purposes. That this fact, however, is not generally known, may be seen from the following statement in Law Notes for November, 1917:

"In the United States marriage by proxy is unknown but it is reported that military necessity has recently led to an analagous expedient, an officer at Camp Mills, L. I., being wedded to a woman in Georgia. There is little question as to the validity of this particular marriage, it being of course assumed that the identity of the parties was properly ascertained. A common-law marriage is valid in both New York and Georgia. But in jurisdictions where an official or ceremonial marriage is requisite some difficulty is presented, as it is very doubtful whether an official transaction can be conducted by telephone. An oath cannot be thus administered. (138 Ga. 1; 169 App. Div. [N. Y.] 469.) Neither may a wife's separate acknowledgment to her husband's deed be taken by telephone. (123 Tenn. 508.) If the practice becomes common it may be necessary to enact a law as to soldiers' marriages analogous to the testamentary privileges now accorded.''

This same article appeared in the Chicago Legal News for October, 1918.

In one of the best of our encylopedias it is stated that

---

[4]Ruling Case Law, Vol. 18, p. 392. The same statement is also made in a note in L. R. A. 1915E, p. 23, on the authority of a dictum of Lord Cranworth in Campbell v. Campbell, L. R. 1, H. L. Sc. App. Cas. 182. In the case of Campbell v. Campbell or the Breadalbane case, decided by the House of Lords in 1867, Lord Cranworth said:

''There is, however, no particular form of ceremony by which such agreement must be manifested, except, indeed, that the parties must, in order to constitute a marriage *de præsenti*, be in the presence of each other when the agreement is entered into, and it must be an agreement to become husband and wife immediately from the time when the mutual consent is given. I do not understand the law as even requiring the presence of a witness as being essential to the validity of a marriage, though, without a witness, it may be difficult to establish it.''

No authority is given for the foregoing dictum. Certainly by the early canon law *sponsalia per verba de præsenti* could be entered into by letter and for stronger reason could *sponsalia per verba de futuro* be entered into although the parties were not in the presence of each other. This is clearly shown by Professor Esmein, the highest authority on marriage in the canon law. *Le Marriage En Droit Canonique* I, p. 169-171 Paris 1891.

"to constitute marriage *per verba de præsenti,* the parties must be in the presence of each other when the agreement is entered into.'" The case of Peck v. Peck, 12 R. I. 485, is cited in support of the statement. This case does not hold anything like that, nor even is there a dictum to that effect.

In an editorial in Law Notes for March, 1919, it was said:

> "There is a report, of doubtful authenticity, that under a new ruling of the War Department American girls may marry American soldiers 'on the Rhine by United States mail. This alleged ruling has been the subject of some derisive comment in the press. The proposition is not as ridiculous as the lay editor seems to think it, but the supposed ruling certainly needs a few qualifications. Of course the question is to be determined by the rules of law; it is not a military matter and the war power at its utmost stretch cannot affect it. In many of the American jurisdictions the assent of parties capable of contracting marriage is all that is required to a valid marriage and that consent need not be signified before any religious or civil celebrant. In such a jurisdiction if two persons exchange letters wherein *per verba de præsenti* they take each other as husband and wife they are legally married."

The War Department did coöperate with many of these couples and below will be seen a copy of the agreement prepared by the office of the Judge Advocate General of the Army which speaks for itself. A number of these marriages were held valid, but of course only where the bride lived in one of the few states where mere consenting words constitutes marriage. Doing this by proxy as is suggested by Professor Lorenzen[5] seems never to have occurred to these couples.

The following is a copy of the agreement above referred to:

This indenture of two parts made, executed, published and declared by and between John Doe of Buffalo in the State of New York serving with the American Expeditionary Forces as Private, Company...... and Mary Roe of Buffalo in the State of New York.

WITNESSETH:

That, whereas heretofore a marriage was intended by said parties to be had between them and each of parties had engaged, promised and agreed with and to the other to make and consummate said marriage, and

Whereas, the said John Doe, being a member of the Army of the United States, was sent beyond seas for service against the public enemy so that said intended marriage could not and cannot be had and solemnized in the usual manner under the ordinary forms, and

Whereas, there exists no legal impediment to the lawful marriage of said parties and,

Whereas, good and sufficient reasons them thereunto moving, the said parties desire to carry their said intention to intermarry into present and immediate effect:

Now therefore, in consideration of the promises and of the mutual and reciprocal covenants and agreements herein and hereby undertaken and made, the said John Doe and the said Mary Roe have covenanted, undertaken and agreed and by these presents do now undertake, covenant and agree, each with the other, and do hereby publish and declare to the world, as follows:

---

[5] 32 Harvard Law Review.

The said John Doe hereby declaring and representing that he was born at Buffalo, New York, January, 1, 1890; that his domiciliary residence is Buffalo, New York; that he is not related by consanguinity or affinity to Mary Roe herein mentioned and that he has no wife other than said Mary Roe does hereby take the said Mary Roe for his true and lawful wife and does hereby acknowledge, declare and publish to the world that said Mary Roe is now henceforth his wife, and he her husband.

And the said Mary Roe hereby declaring and representing that she was born at Buffalo, New York, February 1, 1890; that her domiciliary residence immediately prior to the execution of this indenture was Buffalo, New York; that she is not related by consanguinity of affinity to John Doe herein mentioned, and that she has no husband other than the said John Doe, does hereby take the said John Doe for her true and lawful husband and does hereby acknowledge, declare and publish to the world that said John Doe is now henceforth her husband, and she his wife.

And said husband hereby constitutes and appoints said wife his attorney in fact, with power of substitution, for the purpose of making, doing or obtaining or causing to be made, done or obtained any and all things, acts, licenses, publications, records or assurances, necessary, required or permitted by laws of any State, Territory or District of the United States, for the further, better, more perfect and absolute effecting and assurance of said marriage.

In witness whereof the parties hereto have executed this indenture in duplicate, in presence of the witnesses, named below respectively, the said John Doe in France on the first day of February, 1918 and the said Mary Doe, nee Mary Roe, at Buffalo, N. Y., on the first day of April, 1918.

JOHN DOE (Seal)

WITNESSES:

John Roe, Captain ......
Richard Roe, Private ......
William Roe, Lieut. ......

MARY ROE (Seal)

WITNESSES:

John Brown,
Richard Brown,
William Brown.

A. E. F., France:

Before me, duly constituted and acting as a summary court-martial of the Army of the United States, personally appeared this said day of February, 1918, John Doe, personally known to me to be the identical person he subscribed the foregoing document and acknowledged that he signed, sealed, published and declared the above and foregoing instrument, in duplicate, as his free and voluntary act for the intents and purposes therein, set forth. The said John Doe being then by me first duly sworn did state upon his oath that the recitals, declarations and statements of and concerning himself contained in said instrument are true.

JOHN SMITH, Captain ......
Summary Court Martial.

City of Buffalo,

State of New York, *ss:*

Before me the undersigned Notary Public, personally appeared Mary Roe this first day of April, 1918, known to me to be the identical person who subscribed the foregoing instrument and acknowlegded that she signed, sealed, published and declared the above and foregoing instrument as her free and voluntary act for the intents and purposes therein set forth. The said Mary Roe being then by me first duly sworn did state upon her oath that the recitals, declarations and statements are true.

FRANK ROE,
Notary Public.

(Seal)

Ordinarily, a promise made by mail or telegraph "speaks" to use the language of Mr. Justice Lindley "in the place where it is received. While therefore the place of mailing a letter may impose a liability this must be subject also to the legislative power of the place of receipt, to the extent of affecting the nature of the offer and the instrumentalities both of offer and of receipt."[6] But in the case of American soldiers, as was noted in Law Notes, there is a doubt whether the members of the army of occupation can be said to be in any sense subject to German law or whether any act of theirs which is sanctioned by military law and by the laws of the United States can be invalid because of conflict with the local regulations of Germany. However, many of the "contracts" were sent to the Expeditionary Forces where the man signed it, and then returned it to the United States for signature by the bride.

The general rule as to the law governing these marriages is well stated by Wharton, Conflict of Laws, Vol. I, 369, 3rd Ed. as follows:

> Consensual marriages abroad, by domiciled citizens of states holding such marriages to be valid, will not be invalidated because the forms prescribed in the state of celebration were not adopted, supposing (1) it was impossible to use such forms, or (2) they were repugnant to the religious convictions of the parties or (3) they were not imposed on foreigners by the state prescribing them.

As to the first exception, where the marriage takes place in France, Lawrence in his Commentaries on Wheaton, III, 346 says:

---

[6] 34 Harvard Law Review, 51.

"It would in most cases be impossible for foreigners to comply with the French law. The Code, for instance, requires a prior continued residence of six months in the same commune. The consent of parents is required, and a publication in the domicil of each of the parties. A registry is to be made, presupposing a prior registry of the birth of the parties, and the marriage of their parents, though it would be out of the power of most citizens of the United States to appeal to such a registry."

It has also been held as we have previously seen by a Federal Court in the recent case of G. N. Railway v. Johnson, [254 Fed. 683 (1918)] that it is not necessary for the parties to be in each other's presence when the agreement is executed.

MARRIAGES, PER VERBA DE FUTURO CUM COPULA

In a recent work on marriage and divorce, under the title "Marriage Without a Celebration" it is stated after the definition "a marriage without a celebration is called a common law marriage" that "a promise of marriage at some future time with a mutual understanding that it shall take place is sufficient consent to constitute marriage if consummated by sexual intercourse.'" The case of Cargile v. Wood, 63 Mo. 501, is cited in support of the statement. This statement, if true, is in effect that marriages *per verba de futuro cum copula* are valid. It is believed, however, that an examination of the case will show that the court did not so hold. What the court did hold was that marriage would be inferred from cohabitation and repute. The doctrine of common law marriage is not involved in the case.

7Keezer, Marriage and Divorce p. 27. (1906.)

It is doubtful whether the doctrine is recognized anywhere today. A recent encyclopedia says: "It is a fair
conclusion that the doctrine is nearly, if not quite obso-
lete."[8] Still there is so much dicta in the reports concerning marriage *per verba de futuro* that all writers on
such subjects as Domestic Relations devote some space
to it. The doctrine has, too, been the subject of some
interesting disputes. One recent writer on Domestic Relations says in regard to marriage *per verba de futuro
cum copula:*

> "The old maxim is: *consensus, non concubitas,
> facit nuptias;* and the rule became formulated as
> follows: *consent per verba de præsenti,* with or
> without consummation, constitutes a common law
> marriage; or *consent per verba de futuro,* followed
> by consummation. The latter part of this formula
> has been repeated from time immemorial by text
> writers and in decided cases, and yet it is manifestly
> an incorrect statement of the law. If an agree-
> ment for future marriage followed by cohabitation
> constituted a valid marriage, then every case of
> seduction under promise of marriage would be a
> legal marriage in fact. The true rule is that there
> must be a present consent to enter into the marriage
> relation.* * *"[9]

---

[8]18 Ruling Case Law 394.

[9]Peck, Domestic Relations p. 16. This view was also stated very early
by the Supreme Court of South Carolina in the case of Fryer v. Fryer
(Rich. Equity Cas. 85, 1832) in which the court says:

"Does the copula, *ipso facto*, perfect the previous agreement, so as to
constitute marriage? This, in my opinion, depends entirely upon the
intention and the apprehension of the parties. If an agreement be made
by the Supreme Court of South Carolina in the case of Fryer v. Fryer
coming together shall, *per se*, signify that they have thereby concluded
their contract: there the copula is a performance of the contract, and
by perfecting reduces it from an executory into an executed agreement.
So where there was no express stipulation that the copula should perfect
the previous executory agreement, yet if it be evident that the parties
understood and intended that act to perfect it, I suppose it must have

There are to be found in the reports numerous cases in which the substance of the foregoing is approved. Among them are the oft quoted cases of Cheney v. Arnold (15 N. Y. 345) and Duncan v. Duncan (10 Ohio St. 181) cited by the author of the foregoing statement. Mr. Bishop's criticism of these two decisions is, in the opinion of the present writer, entirely sound. Mr. Bishop says there is nothing in a breach of promise suit or an action for seduction that necessarily militates against the doctrine under consideration. He defines the doctrine and states the correct rule as he sees it as follows:

> "Accurately viewed, the doctrine * * * is a rule of evidence, not of law. But the manner of the books is to treat it in connection with the law, and it would be a practical inconvenience to do otherwise in these volumes.
>
> "The doctrine is, that, if parties who are under an agreement of future marriage have copula, being what is lawful in marriage alone, they are presumed, in the absence of any showing to the contrary, to have arrived at the period of actual marriage, or to have transmuted their future to present promise; because the law accepts the good rather than the evil construction of equivocal acts. Hence, in a form of expression common in the books, one of the methods of contracting marriage is said to be *per verba de futuro cum copula.*

---

that effect. But it is of the essence of every contract that the parties shall have a present contracting intention, at the time of perfecting their contract: they must understand that they are making a contract; otherwise no contract is made. I do not say that they must have a full understanding of the legal consequences of the contract they are forming. The contract once made, the consequences are matter of legal obligation, and they must abide by them. *The proposition contended for, that copula following promises to marry is marriage, without regard to the present intention of the parties, seems to me unfounded in principle. If it were true, there could be no such thing as an action for seduction......*"

"The true view is believed to be, that the copula after promise establishes marriage prima facie, yet no further; that this prima facie case may be rebutted by evidence, for which purpose circumstantial evidence is as good as any other; that thus a question of fact is raised, to be decided on presumption and testimony combined, and this question is, under instructions from the court, for the jury. All the circumstances of the case may be looked into, including the conduct of the parties both before and after the relied-on copula. And if they did not regard themselves after it as married, the marriage presumption is weakened." (Vol. I, secs. 353 *et seq.*) .

There was current English authority for the position taken by Mr. Bishop. Thus in the case of Yelverton v. Longworth, a Scotch appeal decided by the House of Lords in 1863 (4 Macq. H. L. C. 743) it was held that under the law of Scotland a marriage *per verba de futuro cum copula* is effected only where the copula can be connected with the promise. At page 856 the Lord Chancellor (Westbury) said:

"There is but one principle of law, viz., *consensus facit matrimonium.* This may be proved by evidence of the actual exchange of consent, or it may be proved by the aid of a presumption of law. For where there is proof of an antecedent promise of marriage followed by sexual intercourse *which can be referred to the promise,* the Scotch law (if the thing be done in Scotland), furnishes a *presumptio juris et de jure* that at the time of the copula there was an interchange of matrimonial consent in fulfilment; and thus, on the same ground of consensus, declares that which has passed to be *ipsum matrimonium.*"

At page 861 Lord Wensleydale said:

> "Secondly, a promise *per verba de futuro, subsequente copula, connected with that promise, and taking place on the faith of it,* constitutes a valid marriage. To prove that promise, the evidence must be in writing, or it must be proved on the oath of the party against whom the proceeding takes place. The promise must be made in Scotland, but the proof of it may be writing of the party promising made anywhere."

At page 899 Lord Chelmsford said:

> "It cannot be disputed that, in order to constitute a marriage by the combination of a promise with a subsequent copula, *the copula must be clearly and distinctly referable to the promise.*"

At page 902 Lord Kingsdown said:

> "Both the promise and the copula must be in Scotland, and *the copula must be connected with the promise.*"

On the other hand, in the case of Yelverton v. Longworth, a Scotch appeal decided by the House of Lords in 1864, it was urged at the bar as appears at page 822 of the report:

> "Then as to copula; what says Lord Campbell in the Queen v. Millis? (a) He says, 'You must look to the intention of the parties; for if the woman in surrendering her person is conscious that she is committing an act of fornication instead of consummating her marriage, marriage will not thereby be *constituted,*'"

To which Lord Brougham replied:

> "I do not believe that Lord Campbell ever said that the copula must be with the intention of constituting marriage. The law itself refers the copula to the prior promise."

In this connection it is interesting to read the following from Lord Stowell in Dalrymple v. Dalrymple (2 Hagg. Const. 65) which is quoted with approval by Dr. Phillimore in his work on Ecclesiastical Law (2nd Ed., Vol. 1, p. 553):

> "In the promise or *sponsalia de futuro,* nothing was presumed to be complete or consummated either in substance or in ceremony. Mutual consent would release the parties from their engagements, and one party, without the consent of the other, might contract a valid marriage, regularly or irregularly, with another person; but if the parties who have exchanged the promise had carnal intercourse with each other, the effect of that carnal intercourse was to interpose a presumption of present consent at the time of the intercourse, to convert the engagement into an irregular marriage and to produce all the consequences attributable to that species of matrimonial connection."[10]

John Ayliffe, writing in 1734 in his *Parergon Juris Canonici Anglicani* says in regard to the subject:

> "Tho' the Parties betrothed should protest before the Act done, that they did not thereby intend, that the espousals should become Matrimony; yet this Protestation is defeated by the ensuing Act: For by lying together they are presum'd to have swerved from their dishonest Protestation; and so the former Espousals are now presum'd to be honest Matrimony * * *
>
> "And, lastly, Tho' the Man does by Violance carry away the woman, with whom he has con-

---

[10]There are a great number of cases collected in Halkerston's Digest on the Law of Scotland Relating to Marriage (Edinburgh 1831) in which marriages *per verba de futuro cum copula* are held valid, but although it is repeatedly held that the copula implies a present consent and converts the future promise into a present one, it is not clear from these cases that if the copula was not intended to give effect to the previous promise, marriage nevertheless results.

10

tracted Espousal, and has carnal knowledge of her; yet Espousals hereby become Matrimony, according to Paul de Castro * * *'' (p. 250. London 1734.)

Mr. Reeves in his History of English Law says of such marriages:

> "Espousals, when once contracted, so bound the parties, that they could not retract, but each had a *jus matrimonii,* so as to be able to institute a suit for the ecclesiastical judge by censures to compel the other party to consummate the marriage. Indeed, if a *carnalis copula* succeeded, the marriage was completed without more ceremony; for notwithstanding the maxim, that *non concubitus sed consensus facit matrimonium,* the church presumed that by such act the party meant to perform his promise, rather than commit the sin of fornication. *This was a presumption which did not admit any proof to the contrary,* and it could be done away only by shewing that the espousals had before been legally dissolved, or were in themselves null and void. If there were more than one espousals, the former were preferred, even though the latter had been sanctioned by an oath; unless indeed a *carnalis copula* had taken place. The effect of espousals was to create such a relationship, that the *consanguinei* of the *sponsus,* or man espoused, could not, upon his death, or the dissolution of the espousals, marry with the *sponsa,* nor vice versa. (3rd Ed., Vol. IV. 53, 54.)

Although many text writers and American courts have argued that there is no legal justification for the rule *per verba de futuro cum copula* and that the doctrine has been misunderstood, in the opinion of the present writer there is no doubt that the espousal *per verba de futuro cum copula* was recognized as *ipsum matrimonium* by the canon law and that such marriages were recognized as valid by the ecclesiastical courts in England prior to the

Act of 1753. The only question is, what effect was given the copula? In nearly all the books we see in substance that "espousals *de futuro* do become matrimony by carnal knowledge between the parties betrothed." Is this however as maintained by Bishop only a rule of evidence, the copula merely giving rise to a *prima facie* presumption of marriage which must give way to proof that the parties did not intend matrimony at the time of the copula? Also, has this always been the rule? That under the canon law the effect of the copula was to give rise to a presumption of marriage which did not admit of contrary proof has been conclusively shown by Professor Esmein of the University of Paris, the greatest authority on Marriage in the Canon Law. In his *Le Mariage en Droit Canonique* he says:

> "*By the mere fact of the copula carnalis taking place between the parties the agreement was transferred into a true marriage without the need of any manifested consent and without the contrary will of the parties being able to prevent this result from taking place.* This doctrine appears in itself quite strange, whatever explanation was furnished for it by the canonists; but, however, it is explained very well when one cites precedents for it. It is simply a survival of the theory adopted by Gratian and which is maintained here. *Conjugium desponsatione initiatur commixtione perfictur.* Marriage here, as before, presented itself as an act in two tenses. One was able to say *Facit enim pactio conjugalis ut quæ prius erat sponsa in coitu fiat conjux.* In his deductions the doctrine of the decretalist showed itself very faithful to this tradition. It decides in fact that the *copula carnalis* and *sponsalia de futuro* succeeding each other but in the inverse order did not make a marriage. He admitted still that the *coitus* even committed by force on the part

of the man had this transforming effect; and this
was very logical for according to the ancient theory
the *desponsatio* was a marriage in which the *com-
mixtio sexum* only was lacking. The man had the
right to obtain this by any means. The canonists
required only one thing, that is there should have
been something more than attempts at the sexual
relations; they should have been complete and such
that the *unitas carnis* was the consequence thereof.

But this historical explanation, quite naturally,
was not that given by the canonists. They had to
put this rule in accord with the principle henceforth
uncontested, that the essential element for the for-
mation of marriage was the *consensus de præsenti*.
How to establish that, at the moment of the copula,
the parties had the actual will of taking each other
as husband and wife was a difficulty got around by
supposing in their case by legal presumption which
did not admit of contrary proof. Hence they called
these marriages presumptive marriages. They
called attention to the fact that, thanks to this presumption, they took from the copula the character
of fornication which, without this it would necessarily have presented. The effect of this presumption was peremptory in the *forum externum* but
the doctors questioned whether in the *forum inter-
num* the truth would not get the upper hand so that
the same marriage would have to be considered as
valid on one side and null on the other.'"[11]

As has been previously stated the action for seduction
and the doctrine *per verba de futuro cum copula* are not
necessarily inconsistent. In many cases of seduction the
promise of marriage is in consideration of the copula or

[11]*Le Mariage en Droit Canonique* I, p. 142-144. Professor Esmein's
work is undoubtedly the *magnum opus* on the subject. His work, written
a number of years after Bishop's great work on Marriage and Divorce,
has never been translated into English and apparently has not been often
examined by American Courts and text writers. Such learned writers as
Pollock and Maitland, Howard, Lorenzen and other scholarly American
law professors, however, never overlooked Esmein's work.

contingent upon pregnancy. In this respect the copula precedes the time when the promise is effective. Pollock and Maitland are undoubtedly correct in saying that "the scheme at which they (the canonists) thus arrived was certainly no masterpiece of human wisdom. Of all people in the world lovers are the least likely to distinguish precisely between the present and future tenses."[12] But we are dealing here with the law and not with the facts. In those cases, however, where the promise clearly precedes the copula it would seem that the action for seduction and the doctrine under consideration are inconsistent. Mr. Parsons in his work on Contracts has stated the matter very clearly and accurately, and so far as his statement goes we accept it. His statement is as follows:

"It may be remarked, that the practice of the courts in this country, in one respect, seems directly opposed to the rule that "if the contract be made *per verba de futuro,* and be followed by consummation, it amounts to a valid marriage, and is equally binding as if made *in facie ecclesiæ.*" For a very large proportion of the cases in which an action is brought for breach of promise of marriage come within this definition. The man promised marriage, the woman accepted and returned the promise, and thereupon yielded to his wishes. It is a question, which we have already considered, how far the seduction may be given in evidence, in this section, to swell the damages; but in some way or other, if the fact exists, it is usually brought out. Then it becomes a case of marriage, if it be indeed law that an agreement to marry, *per verba de futuro,* followed by consummation, constitutes marriage. *But such a defense was never made by the party, nor interposed by the court.* It is true that the man would not be likely to make this defense, for

[12]History of English Law Bk. II, p. 367.

that would be to acknowledge himself the husband
of the plaintiff. But if, in such an action, it should
appear that the parties had celebrated a regular
marriage, *in facie ecclesiæ,* and were unquestionably
husband and wife, certainly the court would not
wait for the defendant to avail himself of that fact,
but as soon as it was clearly before them would
stop the case. For if they were once married, no
agreement of both parties, and no waiver of both
or either, would annul the marriage. *And the cir-
cumstance that this objection is never made, where
it appears that there was a mutual promise and
subsequent cohabitation, would go far to show that
the courts of this country do not regard such a contract, although followed by consummation, as equivalent to a marriage in which the formalities sanctioned by law or usage are observed."* (8th Ed.
p. 85.)

Marriages *per verba de futuro cum copula* have never
been expressly recognized in a single one of the states,
although, as we have seen, the books abound with ill
considered dicta to the effect that they are valid. Informal marriage, valid at common law, then is not fully
recognized in any state in the union and, as will be seen
from the table in the next chapter, is not even partially
valid in the great majority of states. What we have in
many states is an entirely different doctrine under the
name "common-law marriage."

PROOF OF MARRIAGE FROM COHABITATION AND REPUTE

The rule that a marriage may be proved by cohabitation is, indeed, often confused with the doctrine of common law marriage. This we have already noted inci-
dentally. In the Russell Sage Foundation's Compilation
of American Marriage Laws, published in 1919, appears
the following:

"But another judicial decision in Maryland has given them sanction in practice by use of a legal fiction which the lay mind finds it hard to fathom. In the decision referred to it is stated that 'there cannot be a valid marriage without a religious ceremony; but marriage can be proved by general reputation, cohabitation and acknowledgment, and when these exist it will be inferred that a religious ceremony has taken place, although evidence may not be obtained of the time, place and manner of the celebration. Richardson v. Smith, 80 Md. 89.' "

Again in the same work it is stated at page 32:

"Maryland is classed here as recognizing such marriages in practice, in spite of the fact that technically the ruling is that a recognition is denied."

Again at page 79 in the same work it is stated:

"Common law, or nonceremonial marriages, are technically not recognized, for it has been held that no marriage is valid without some sort of religious ceremony; but practically such marriages are recognized, for in the same decision it was held that a marriage may be proved by general reputation, cohabitation and acknowledgment and when these exist it will be inferred that a religious ceremony has taken place, although evidence may not be obtained of the time, place and manner of the celebration. We are advised, however, that in prosecutions for bigamy and adultery, and in civil action for criminal conversation, the evidence of general reputation and cohabitation is not sufficient."

The decision above referred to in no wise recognizes the doctrine of common law marriages. It is simply the rule which prevails almost everywhere. The facts in that case are as follows:

Isabella Richardson, by her petition in the orphan's court of Baltimore County, alleged that she is the widow of William Richardson, who died intestate, and, that without notice to her, letters of administration on his estate have been granted to his sister, Eliza A. Smith. The petitioner prays that the letters may be revoked, and that she may have general relief. Eliza A. Smith answered the petition and denied that the petitioner was the widow, and that she was ever the wife of the deceased. The petitioner prayed an issue in the following terms: "Whether the petitioner, Isabella Richardson, is the widow of William Richardson, deceased." The orphans' court refused to grant the issue proposed in behalf of the petitioner and ordered the three following: 1st issue; "Was William Richardson, late of Baltimore County, deceased, married to Isabella Parsons; and if yea, when, where, and how was said marriage celebrated? 2nd issue; Was William Richardson the husband of said Isabella Parsons at the time of his death, to wit, December 10, 1893? 3rd issue; Was Isabella Parsons the wife of William Richardson at the time of his death, to wit, December 10, 1893?"

The court did say at page 93:

"In this state there cannot be a valid marriage without a religious ceremony, but a marriage may be competently proved without the testimony of witnesses who were present at the ceremony. It would work very cruel injustice in many instances, if the law were otherwise. The witnesses might be dead, and competent written evidence of the ceremony might be unobtainable. It would not follow, however, that the union between the parties would be considered illicit and the children illegitimate. The law has wisely provided that marriage may be proved by general reputation, cohabitation and acknowledgment; when these exist, it will be inferred that a religious ceremony has taken place; and this proof will not be invalidated because evidence cannot be obtained of the time, place and manner of the celebration of the marriage."

In support of the above statement the court cited a number of authorities to show where parties live together ostensibly as man and wife, demeaning themselves toward each other as such, and are received into society and treated by their friends and relations as having and being entitled to that status, the law will, in favor of morality and decency presume that they have been legally married and that, indeed, the most usual way of proving marriage except in actions for criminal conversation and in prosecutions for bigamy is by general reputation, cohabitation and acknowledgment. It must be observed that the rule followed by the Maryland court is in no sense a conclusive presumption. It is a presumption prevailing everywhere, the effect of which is that where parties are living together as husband and wife the law will presume that the relation existing between them is legal rather than illegal. The *maxim semper præsumitur pro matrimonio* is well established in our law. Of course, if the parties admit that they have never been married according to the law of the particular state the presumption fails. And so in the Maryland case, the petitioner claimed a marriage in accordance with the law of the state. Otherwise the decision would have been against her.

And the distinction discussed above has also been overlooked by one of the most learned writers on the subject. Professor Howard says:

> "The contract by mere present consent of the parties regardless of the statutory requirements, has been widely accepted as valid in the group of southern and southwestern states and territories. It was so judicially accepted....in the District of Columbia in 1865. Blackburn v. Crawford, 3 Wall. 175; Diggs v. Wormley, 21 D. C. 477; Jennings v.

Webb, 8 App. D. C. 43; Green v. Norment, 5 Mackey 80.''

An examination of the cases cited by him shows that in all cases the question was not the validity of a marriage by mere present consent of the parties but only the presumption of marriage from cohabitation and repute.[18] That the validity of such marriages is in doubt in the District of Columbia has been elsewhere pointed out.

After reading the above from Professor Howard, the following from Moore's Digest of International Law seems curious indeed. It illustrates what has been already maintained, that the subject has not been given the investigation it deserves.

> "The requisites of a valid marriage in the different states and territories are sometimes matters of judicial ascertainment, as well as of statutory enactment. For example, Circular No. 39, in giving the requisites of a valid marriage in Massachusetts, wholly omits to state what has *since* been decided by the Supreme Judicial Court of that Commonwealth, that a consensual marriage, without the presence of an officiating clergyman or magistrate, and to which neither party was a Friend or Quaker, is invalid. (Commonwealth v. Munson, 127 Mass. 459.) *It has also recently been held in the District of Columbia that a marriage in the District by consent, without some religious ceremony, is not sufficient to make a valid marriage by the law there existing.*[14]

---

[18]History Matrimonial Institutions, III, p. 176.

[14]Vol. II, p. 532. Secy. of State Bayard to Mr. McLane, May 9, 1887. Not only is it error concerning the District of Columbia but it leaves an incorrect inference regarding Massachusetts. The word ''since'' would indicate that the decision of Com. v. Munson changed the law of that state. As we have seen common law marriages have never been valid in Massachusetts and this the Supreme Court of that state has repeatedly held since 1810.

COMMON LAW MARRIAGE AFTER THE REMOVAL OF THE IMPEDIMENT

The general rule in a State recognizing common law marriage is that the continued cohabitation of the parties after the removal of the impediment to a valid ceremonial marriage constitutes a valid common law marriage, and in a few jurisdictions marriages under such circumstances are recognized, although common law marriages as such are invalid. There need be no new agreement between the parties to be henceforth husband and wife; the mere continued cohabitation after the removal of the impediment is alone sufficient.

Some courts have held that the mere continued cohabitation of the parties after the removal of the impediment does not constitute marriage where the cohabitation in its inception was meretricious. This is founded on the legal presumption that cohabitation originally illicit so continues until the contrary intent is shown.

When the proof shows that the cohabitation was in its origin meretricious, that is, that the parties were consciously living in a state of fornication and without any pretense of marriage, the rule is given full effect, though there appears to be some difference of opinion as to the nature of the proof necessary to overthrow the presumption. The principal difficulty arises in cases where the parties evidently desired matrimony and did everything in their power to effect their desire, as evidenced by a marriage agreement or solemnized marriage, which, however, was void because of the fact that one or both of the parties had a husband or wife living and undivorced, or marriage was otherwise prohibited. In such cases it is, of course, imperative that a marital agreement should have been entered into by the parties after the removal of the impediment, but some of the courts have insisted on evidence from which an express agreement could be implied, and have refused to imply such an agreement from evidence of a continuance of the cohabitation of the parties after the removal of the impediment. Some courts, following this view, have applied the presumption as to illicit cohabitation and have treated the cohabitation as meretricious in law, especially where one of the parties had knowledge of the impediment. Others have emphasized the ignorance of one of the parties of the existence of the impediment and of its removal as evidence rebutting any implication of an express agreement. Even such jurisdictions, however, are inclined to find a common-law marriage where it appears that both parties were ignorant of the impediment and acted in good faith in contracting the void marriage.

On the other hand, the weight of authority seems to be that if the parties desired and intended matrimony, as distinguished from a mutually meretricious relationship, and such desire and intent continued after the removal of the impediment, as evidenced by a continuation of the cohabitation in the apparent relationship of husband and wife, the parties are to be deemed married as soon as the impediment is removed.

This rule is more than a rule of evidence. It amounts to a holding that the marriage relation can be created without an express agreement, but from cohabitation alone where it appears that such cohabitation was entered upon with the desire and intent for matrimony. Knowledge by one or both of the parties of the existence of the impediment becomes immaterial, except as it may affect the question of the desire and intent of the parties. There are numerous cases which have upheld the marriage where one of the parties must have known of the impediment, and several in which knowledge by both parties was disclosed by the evidence. Other courts, however, while subscribing to the general rule, have refused to apply it where it appeared that both parties were conscious of the unlawfulness of the relationship.

As has been stated, the authorities are in great conflict in regard to this phase of the subject. They vary all the way from the strict rule in force in Illinois to the extremely liberal rule adopted in Ohio. In the case of Johnson v. Dudley, 3 Ohio N. P. 196, a valid common law marriage was found between a white man and a colored woman who had moved to Ohio from Alabama where such marriages were made criminal. The holding of the court is well summarized as follows in the syllabus:

> "A marriage may be proved from acts of recognition, cohabitation, birth of children, and the like, and this even when the parties originally came together under a void contract, and also where the intercourse was at the commencement illicit. And in the case of conflicting presumptions on the subject of legitimacy, that in favor of innocence must prevail."

An interesting question is presented where a man and a woman are living together under a void ceremonial marriage in a State where common law marriages are

not recognized, but later move to a State in which they
are recognized, without in any way evidencing an intent
to create a valid common law marriage.   Perhaps they
may even be ignorant of the illegality of their ceremonial
marriage.   Does their continued cohabitation in the State
where common law marriages are valid constitute a marriage, and if so, how long must they cohabit in such a
State in order to create a common law marriage?

In the case of Travers v. Reinhart, 205 U. S. 423,
Travers and a woman named Sophia entered into what
she thought was a valid ceremonial marriage in Virginia
in 1865.   This marriage was performed without a license
and by a person who had no authority to perform a
marriage ceremony and was consequently void in Virginia, a State in which common law marriages are not
recognized.   The parties moved to Maryland and there
lived for fifteen years, where common law marriages are
not recognized.   They then moved to New Jersey, where
they lived for six months when Travers died and litiga-
tion involving the validity of his marriage was instituted.
The court held there was a valid common law marriage
in New Jersey.   The court said:

> "We are of opinion that even if the alleged mar-
> riage would have been regarded as invalid in Vir-
> ginia for want of license, had the parties remained
> there, and invalid in Maryland for want of a re-
> ligious ceremony, had they remained in that state,
> it was to be deemed a valid marriage in New Jersey
> after James Travers and the woman Sophia, as
> husband and wife, took up their permanent resi-
> dence there and lived together in that relation, con-
> tinuously, in good faith, and openly, up to the death
> of Travers, being regarded by themselves and in
> the community as husband anl wife.   Their conduct

toward each other in the eye of the public, while in
New Jersey, taken in connection with their previous
association, was equivalent, in law, to a declaration
by each that they did and during their joint lives
were to occupy the relation of husband and wife.
Such declaration was as effective to establish the
status of marriage in New Jersey as if it had been
made in words of the present tense after they became domiciled in that state.''

It might be inferred from this decision of the Supreme
Court that the domicile of the parties in New Jersey
was important. We believe, however, that this is of no
consequence whatever. It is not necessary that the parties be domiciled in a State in order to contract a valid
marriage there. The mere presence of the persons in
the State, provided they can comply with the require-
ments in the State, is sufficient. The rule is stated by
Professor Long in his work on Domestic Relations at Section 78 as follows:

''It is a rule of universal recognition that a marriage valid where celebrated is valid everywhere
and this rule applies not only to the marriages of
persons domiciled in places where the marriage was
celebrated, but also where the parties are mere so-
journers in such place.''

The rule is also very clearly set forth by Bishop in his
great work on Marriage, Divorce and Separation in Sec-
tions 838-843 as follows:

''Marriage being a universal right, and there
being one law of marriage governing all nations
alike, subject only to mere local and not extrater-
ritorial regulations of the State wherein it is celebrated, if, at any place where parties may be,
whether transiently or permanently, they enter into
what by the law of the place is a marriage, they

will be holden everywhere else throughout Christendom to be husband and wife."

In Section 843 it is stated:

"By the international law of marriage, which
ought to govern the courts in the absence of any
statute of their own forbidding, a marriage valid
by the law of the Country in which it is celebrated,
though the parties are but transient persons, though
it would be invalid entered into under the same
formalities in the place of their domicil, and even
though contracted in express evasion of their own
law, is good everywhere.   And this doctrine is
specifically established in the tribunals of the common-law countries."

Suppose the parties in that case had lived together in
New Jersey but one day.   Upon principle should not the
decision have been the same?   The Supreme Court of
Massachusetts has held that the cohabitation in New
York for a short time of persons domiciled in Massachusetts who were living together in an illegal relationship
in Massachusetts does not constitute a common law marriage valid in New York which is valid in Massachusetts.
The court said:

"The substance of what was proved is that the
parties, without being married, were living together as husband and wife in Massachusetts, and
while doing so they twice went to New York together, and continued in the same apparent relation,
—at one time for three days, and at another for
one week.   We have not been referred to any decision in New York which holds that these facts
would either constitute marriage there, or afford
a conclusive presumption of it; and we are slow
to believe that acts which in Massachusetts were
illicit will be deemed matrimonial merely by being
continued without any new sanction by residents of

Massachusetts while transiently across the state line." (Norcross v. Norcross, 155 Mass. 425.)

In the recent case of Rowland v. United States in the United States District Court at East St. Louis, Illinois, in which the writer represented the United States, a marriage valid in Illinois was found between persons who were living together in Illinois under a void ceremonial marriage, but who went to Ohio where common law marriages are recognized (for a period of three months) and returned to Illinois, where common law marriages are not recognized.

The following appears in the court's findings of fact and conclusions of law in the Rowland case:

> "During September 1913 said Fred Rowland and Ruth Stokes Rowland, more than a year and a half after the aforesaid divorce of aforesaid Fred Rowland removed to the State of Ohio and there lived in the relation of, and held themselves out to the world as husband and wife, until during the month of December 1913, when they returned to the State of Illinois.
>
> "The conduct of the said Fred Rowland and Ruth Stokes Rowland in so living together in the relation of husband and wife, holding themselves out to the world as husband and wife, he introducing her into society and to his friends as his wife and she, likewise recognizing him as her husband during the said period from September to December 1913 inclusive, constituted under the laws of the State of Ohio a common-law marriage and he was her common-law husband and she his common-law wife.
>
> "Under the foregoing facts the court finds as a conclusion of law that Ruth Stokes Rowland is

the lawful widow of Fred Rowland and that Genevive Rowland is the legitimate child of said Fred Rowland.''[15]

This phase of the subject is in a hopeless condition. On principle the time element should not enter into the question. The rule is that if the parties enter into what by the law of the place, is a marriage, whether they be there transiently or permanently, they are married. Therefore, if the mere continued cohabitation after the removal of the impediment to a valid ceremonial marriage, constitutes a valid common law marriage, it would seem that if the parties desire and intend matrimony and merely pass through a jurisdiction recognizing common law marriage, a valid common law marriage would be created by the mere fact that they went through such jurisdiction, even perhaps on a sleeping car, without ever knowing it.

---

[15]In Evatt v. Miller, 114 Ark. 84, it was held that a common law marriage contracted in Texas, and valid under that law, will be treated as valid in Arkansas in which state common law marriages are not recognized.

CHAPTER IX

The tabular analysis which follows agrees for the most part with the table prepared by the Russell Sage Foundation in 1919. There are some important exceptions, however, which should be noted. In the Russell Sage Foundation Compilation, Oregon is listed as a state where common law marriages are invalid. I have listed common law marriages as probably valid in Oregon. The Supreme Court of that state has never squarely passed on the point. In one case there is dictum, however, to the effect that a marriage *per verba de præsenti* is valid. (Estate of Megenson, 21 Ore. 387.) On the other hand, there is a dictum of the United States Circuit Court for the District of Oregon that common law marriages are not valid in that state. This statement was entirely unnecessary and cannot be considered as the law of the state. It is clearly contrary to the decision of the United States Supreme Court in Meister v. Moore, 96 U. S. 76. The dictum of the United States Circuit Court is further discredited by the fact that the judge also incorrectly stated the law of California existing at that time. The United States Board of Pension Appeals has held that for the purposes of the Pension Bureau a common law marriage contracted in Oregon is valid. (18 Pension

Dec. 323.) The same rule has been followed by the Bureau of War Risk Insurance.[1]

In the Russell Sage Foundation Compilation, New Hampshire is listed as a state where common law marriages are recognized as valid by statute but with certain qualifications. The qualifications are not stated. Common law marriages have not been valid in New Hampshire since 1849. (Dunbarton v. Franklin, 19 N. H. 257.) The statute closely follows the Massachusetts statute, and the Massachusetts rule has been approved and followed. There is a presumption of marriage from cohabitation where parties cohabit and acknowledge each other as husband and wife and are generally reputed to be such for a period of three years and until the decease of one of them, but this is not a recognition of the doctrine of common law marriage.

The Russell Sage Foundation Compilation also classes Maryland as a state recognizing common law marriages as valid, which, in the opinion of the present writer is clearly erroneous. This, however, is discussed elsewhere.

In the Sage Foundation Compilation six states are given as doubtful. I state but one to be doubtful, the District of Columbia. Much may be said both for and against this statement as to the District of Columbia. The common law of the District of Columbia is that of Maryland at the date the District was created, while on

---

[1]Mr. Hall of the Russell Sage Foundation very kindly wrote me November 14, 1921 advising me of a statement in the Portland, Oregon, Journal, of October 12, 1921, that Circuit Judge Stapleton in the case of Fred O. Twigger v. Martha Twigger directly passed upon the question for the first time in the history of the state, sustaining the validity of common law marriages in Oregon.

the other hand the marriage statute in force in the District is not mandatory.

The Sage Foundation lists Connecticut, Delaware and Maine as doubtful, but probably invalid; District of Columbia, New Mexico and Wyoming as doubtful, but probably valid. I agree that common law marriages are not valid in Connecticut but do not think it is very doubtful. The statute is very mandatory. The United States Board of Pension Appeals has held they were not valid in Connecticut in 1880. (In Re Sarah A. Bartlett, 15 Pension Dec. 290.) The Supreme Court of Delaware has recently held that common law marriages are not valid in that State. I do not believe the question is very doubtful in Maine. The statute is similar to the Massachusetts statute from which it was taken and the Supreme Court of Maine has approved the Massachusetts case of Milford v. Worcester. (Gardiner v. Manchester, 88 Me. 249; 33 Atl. 990.) The statute of New Mexico does not seem to be more mandatory than the statutes of other states which have been held to be directory only. The Attorney General of New Mexico advises that in his opinion such marriages are valid in that state. Little doubt appears as to Wyoming. It has been held that the statute is merely directory, (5 Wyoming 433). And it seems from the case of Weidenhoft v. Primm, (16 Wyoming 34) that such marriages will be recognized.

The following statement in regard to marriages simply *per verba de præsenti* is taken from the Harvard Law Review:

"On principle and by the better view of the authorities, if the parties exchange, whether written or oral promises, to presently assume the status of husband and wife, this agreement without more creates a valid marriage. But there are cases squarely holding that cohabitation is also essential. However unfortunate these latter decisions, they will probably be followed in the states in which they were rendered, and must be given appropriate consideration with our main problem."[2]

We will not discuss whether these decisions were fortunate or unfortunate but invite a careful study of the following tabular analysis which shows that there are also but few cases holding the other way. Therefore, the statement is not entirely fair. What the great majority of states will do when the question of marriage by mere consenting words alone is presented remains to be seen.

THE LAW BY STATES

STATE OR TERRITORY	Per verba de presenti without cohabitation	Per verba de presenti followed by cohabitation	Per verba de futuro cum copula	Presumption of, from cohabitation after removal of impediment
Alabama	invalid c	valid c	invalid c	yes c
Alaska	invalid s	invalid s	invalid s	yes s
Arizona	invalid s	invalid s	invalid s	no s
Arkansas	invalid c	invalid c	invalid c	no c
California	invalid s	invalid s	invalid s	no s
Colorada	invalid c	valid c	invalid c	yes
Connecticut	invalid c	invalid c	invalid c	no c
Delaware	invalid c	invalid c	invalid c	no c
Dist. of Col.	doubtful n	doubtful n	invalid n	doubtful n
Florida	doubtful n	valid c	invalid n	yes n
Georgia	doubtful c	valid c	doubtful c	yes c
Hawaii	invalid n	valid c	invalid n	yes n
Idaho	invalid s	valid s	invalid s	yes c
Illinois	invalid s	invalid s	invalid s	no s

(s) By statute; (n) No decision on the question; (c) By court decision.

[2] 32 H. L. R. 850, May, 1919.

STATE OR TERRITORY	Per verba de præsenti without cohabitation	Per verba de præsenti followed by cohabitation	Per verba de futuro cum copula	Presumption of, from cohabitation after removal of impediment
Indiana	doubtful n	valid c	invalid n	yes c
Iowa	doubtful n	valid c	invalid n	yes s
Kansas	invalid n	valid c	invalid n	yes c
Kentucky	invalid s	invalid s	invalid s	no s
Louisiana	invalid s	invalid s	invalid s	no s
Maine	invalid n	invalid n	invalid n	no n
Maryland	invalid c	invalid c	invalid c	no c
Massachusetts	invalid c	invalid c	invalid c	yes s
Michigan	invalid c	valid c	invalid c	yes c
Minnesota	valid c	valid c	doubtful n	yes c
Mississippi	valid s	valid s	doubtful n	yes n
Missouri	invalid s	invalid s	invalid s	no s
Montana	invalid s	valid s	invalid s	yes n
Nebraska	doubtful c	valid c	doubtful c	yes c
Nevada	doubtful n	valid c	invalid n	yes c
New Hampshire	invalid c	invalid c	invalid c	no c
New Jersey	doubtful n	valid c	invalid n	yes c
New Mexico	doubtful n	valid n	invalid n	yes n
New York	valid c	valid c	invalid c	yes c
North Carolina	invalid s	invalid s	invalid s	no s
North Dakota	invalid s	invalid s	invalid s	no s
Ohio	doubtful n	valid c	invalid n	yes c
Oklahoma	invalid n	valid c	invalid n	doubtful c
Oregon	doubtful c	valid n	invalid n	doubtful n
Pennsylvania	doubtful c	valid c	doubtful c	yes c
Philippine Is.	invalid s	invalid s	invalid s	no s
Porto Rico	invalid s	invalid s	invalid s	no s
Rhode Island	doubtful n	valid n	doubtful c	doubtful n
South Carolina	doubtful c	valid c	doubtful c	yes c
South Dakota	invalid s	valid s	invalid s	doubtful n
Tennessee	invalid c	invalid c	invalid c	no c
Texas	invalid c	valid c	invalid c	yes c
Utah	invalid s	invalid s	invalid s	no s
Vermont	invalid c	invalid c	invalid c	no c
Virginia	invalid s	invalid s	invalid s	no s
Washington	invalid s	invalid s	invalid s	no s
West Virginia	invalid s	invalid s	invalid s	no s
Wisconsin	invalid s	invalid s	invalid s	no s
Wyoming	doubtful n	valid n	invalid n	yes n

(s) By statute; (n) No decision on the question; (c) By court decision.

RECAPITULATION

	Per verba de praesenti without cohabitation	Per verba de praesenti followed by cohabitation	Per verba de futuro cum copula	Presumption of, from cohabitation after removal of impediment
Valid by statute....	1	4	0	3
*Valid by decision...	2	23	0	22
Invalid by statute..	19	17	19	15
*Invalid by decision.	16	8	27	2
Doubtful	15	1	7	5

*This includes the few cases where there is no statute but no positive decision has been made. In each case, however, because of *dicta* or otherwise, there is sufficient reason for not listing it as doubtful.

The books abound with inaccurate statements in regard to the subject which show that it has not been given the attention it deserves. James Bryce in his revised edition of American Commonwealth says that there is little diversity in the laws of marriage in the different states, "the rule everywhere prevailing that no special ceremony is requisite, and the statutory forms not being deemed imperative." This statement is very misleading if not untrue. In the Harvard Law Review for March, 1919, it is stated in two different articles that "in the *great majority* of states the common law marriage is still valid, notwithstanding modern statutes relating to marriage." We have already seen that common law marriages are valid, not in the great majority of states but in only 27 of our 53 states and territories, and this too when we list but one state as doubtful.

Conclusion

At the first conference of the Committee on Uniform State Laws of the American Bar Association in 1892 the following resolution was adopted:

> "Resolved that it be recommended to the State Legislatures that legislation be adopted requiring some ceremony or formality, or written evidence, signed by the parties, and attested by one or more witnesses, in all marriages; provided, however, that in all states where the so-called common law marriage, or marriage without ceremony, is now recognized as valid, no such marriage, hereafter contracted, shall be valid unless evidenced by a writing signed in duplicate by the parties, and attested by at least two witnesses."

By section XXIII of the act recommended by the Commissioners on Uniform State Laws in 1911 for adoption in all the states common law marriages are abolished.

All learned writers on marriage, agree that common law marriages should be declared void.

Howard says:

> "No doubt our common law marriage is thoroughly bad, involving social evils of the most dangerous character."[2]
>
> "Practically all the hardship and social anarchy of the canon law at its wickedest survives in our common law marriage, * * * a custom which legalizes and virtually invites impulsive, impure and secret unions."[3]

Goodsell says:

> "Is it not an amazing fact that, in a matter which so profoundly affects the dignity and stability of a family institution, society should be so slow to take enlightened action? Surely no legislative re-

[2] History of Matrimonial Institutions, Vol. III, p. 171.
[3] Ibid. V, p. 222.

form is more needed than clear and positive statutes declaring such loosely contracted unions null
and void.''[4]

Cook says:

"The law makes clear and full provisions for
contracts affecting the sale of houses and lands,
horses and dogs, and goods and chattels of every
description; and why marriage, the most important
of all human contracts should not be as anxiously
defined and provided for and thus placed beyond
the reach of both fraud and doubt appears to me
to be one of the greatest anomalies in the law of a
Christian country. These are the words of an
eminent Scotch lawyer, with reference to the law
of Scotland. They equally apply to the common
law of the United States.''[5]

"It is certainty and simplicity, then, at which
first of all the states should aim in dealing with
this subject. In the words of Mr. Boyd Kinnear,
an eminent English barrister, the law of the marriage celebration should 'embrace the maximum of
simplicity and the maximum of certainty; of simplicity, because it affects every class, and almost
every person, the most humble and illiterate as
well as the most exalted or learned, and because it
has to be known and acted on in the absence not
only of legal advice, but often in the absence of
even ordinary common-sense counsel; of certainty,
because it affects a contract and social relation the
most important that can arise between human be-
ings—because it affects the foundation of society
itself, and influences the fate, it may be the eternal
fate, of innumerable individuals' * * * Our pre-
dominant common law * * does contain the element
of simplicity. * * * At the same time, what form is
more repugnant to the certainty of the fact of the
parties' consent, and hence is more objectionable
for the practice of a civilized community? In short,

[4]The Family as a Social and Educational Institution, p. 537.
[5]61 Atlantic Monthly, p. 249.

certainty is not to be obtained without publicity, and hence the common law must be repealed.''[6]

In this connection we also read the following from the Supreme Court of Missouri in 1891 in the case of State v. Bittick (11 L. R. A. 587):

> "We will add that we have come to this conclusion very reluctantly, for we feel that the best interests of men and women, and children, of society, of the family and the home require that parties should not 'marry themselves,' and all marriages should be entered into publicly before those authorized by law to solemnize them, and put upon the public records."

Even Pollock and Maitland, the greatest of English legal historians, from whom we would not expect any unjust criticism of English law, say in regard to the canon law rules of marriage:

> "The one contract which, to our thinking, *should certainly be formal,* had been made the most formless of all contracts" (Hist. Eng. Law II, 369).

In a case in which the common law marriage was rejected the Supreme Court of Arkansas said:

> "We have made our decision after mature deliberation, and a careful consideration of the authorities bearing on the subject believing that the views we have expressed and adopted are in accord with the whole system of our marriage laws, and will best foster and protect the home, and promote the sacredness of the marriage relation, which is the foundation of the family and the origin of all forms of government." (Furth v. Furth, 97 Ark. 278.)

The proper attitude in regard to such marriages has been well stated by Professor Bowne, one of America's greatest philosophers, in his work on Ethics as follows:

---

[6]*Ibid.* p. 681.

"Marriage is not a socially indifferent thing. The married couple need the recognition and assistance of society; and society in turn has the right to demand a specific announcement of the relation it has expected and recognized. Hence, the various forms of marriage ceremony. * * *" (Bowne, Principles of Ethics, 236.)

We have but one suggestion to make in connection with this proposed reform. The statutes should provide that where the parties attempt a valid ceremonial marriage, but because of an existing impediment can effect no legal marriage, and continue the marital relationship after the impediment is removed, they should be deemed to be legally married effective from the date the impediment is removed. Alaska, Iowa and Massachusetts seem to be the only jurisdictions in which such provision has been made. Section 14 of the Alaska Act of May 3, 1917, in effect August 1, 1917, provides as follows:

"If a person during the lifetime of a husband or wife with whom the marriage is in force, enters into a subsequent marriage contract in accordance with the provisions of section one (1) of this act, and the parties thereto live together thereafter as husband and wife, and such subsequent marriage contract was entered into by one of the parties in good faith, in the full belief that the former husband or wife was dead, or that the former marriage had been annulled, or dissolved by a divorce, or without knowledge of such former marriage, they shall, after the impediment to their marriage has been removed by death, or divorce of the other party to such former marriage, if they continue to live together as husband and wife in good faith on the part of one of them, be held, to have been legally married from and after the removal of such impediment, and the issue of such subsequent marriage shall be considered as the legitimate issue of both parents.''

Section 3151 of the Iowa Code of 1897 provides as follows:

> "A marriage between persons prohibited by law, or between persons either of whom has a husband or wife living, is void, but if the parties live and cohabit together after the death or divorce of the former husband or wife, such marriage shall be valid." (C. '73, Sec. 2201.)

By the Massachusetts act of May 29, 1895 (R. L. sec. 6, p. 1346), parties to a marriage, void because of the existence of an impediment, may, under certain circumstances, be deemed to be legally married from and after the removal of the impediment. The text of the statute is as follows:

> "If a person during the lifetime of a husband or wife with whom the marriage is in force, enters into a subsequent contract with due legal ceremony and the parties thereto live together thereafter as husband and wife, and such subsequent marriage contract was entered into by one of the parties in good faith, in the full belief that the former husband or wife was dead, that the former marriage had been annulled by divorce, or without knowledge of such former marriage, they shall, after the impediment has been removed by the death or divorce of the other party to the former marriage, if they continue to live together as husband and wife in good faith on the part of one of them, be held to have been legally married from and after the removal of such impediment, and the issue of such subsequent marriage shall be considered as the legitimate issue of both parents."

In the case of a formal marriage, we agree with Mr. Bishop that "where parties are living together, wishing and believing themselves to be husband and wife, if an impediment today prevents the legal status from being superinduced thereby, and tomorrow it is removed, there is reason to hold that the status uprises as the impediment sinks.''

BIBLIOGRAPHY

The less important works consulted will not appear in this list; where they have been helpful, they are cited at the bottom of the pages in the notes. The more important works consulted are given below.

Mariage En Droit Canonique, Esmein, Paris, 1887.

A History of Matrimonial Institutions, 3 volumes, George Elliott Howard, University of Chicago Press, 1904.

Primitive Marriage, Studies in Ancient History, J. F. McLennan, London, 1886.

History of English Law, Pollock and Maitland.

Ancient Law, Sir Henry Maine, New York, 1878.

Domestic Relations, Fraser.

Marriage, Divorce and Separation, Bishop.

Historical Jurisprudence, Guy Carleton Lee.

Marriage and Divorce Laws of the World, Hyacinthe Ringrose.

Commentaries on American Law, James Kent.

Marriage and Divorce, From Studies in History and Jurisprudence, James Bryce.

First Book of Jurisprudence, Pollock.

Canons and Decrees of the Council of Trent. Theodore A. Buckley, London, 1851.

Westermarck's History of Human Marriage, New York, 1891.

The Divorce of Catherine of Aragon, James Froude, New York, 1891.

Clandestine Marriages, Henry Gally, London, 1730.

First Book of Jurisprudence, Pollock, London, 1896.

A Treatise on Spousals, or Matrimonial Contracts, Henry Swinburne, London, 1686.

Marriage and Divorce in the United States, D. Convers, Philadelphia, 1889.

The Marriage Celebration, Four Articles, Frank Gaylord Cook, 61 Atlantic Monthly, 1888.

A Short History of Rhode Island, George W. Greene, Providence, 1877.

History of New England, J. G. Palfrey, 5 Volumes, Boston, 1889.

Domestic Relations, Tapping Reeve, 4th Ed., 1888.

Domestic Relations, James Schouler.

Domestic Relations, Eversly, William Pinder, London, 1885.

A Treatise on Evidence, Simon Greenleaf, 16th Ed., Boston, 1899.

Magnalia Christi Americana: or the Ecclesiastical History of New England, Cotton Mather, Hartford, 1820.

A Short History of Marriage, Tennessee Claflin, 141 Westminster Rev.

Commentaries on The Laws of England, Sir William Blackstone.

Select Essays in Anglo American Legal History, 3 Volumes.

Note on Common Law Marriage, Volume 17 British Ruling Cases.

Note on Common Law Marriage, L. R. A., 1915E.

Note on Common Law Marriage, 124 American State Reports.

Marriage Laws and The Council of Trent, 47 Canadian Law Journal, 481-491 (1911).

Marriage in Roman Law (Stocquart) 16 Yale Law Journal, 303 (1907).

Effect of Removal of Impediment, 28 Yale Law Journal, 515-516 (1919).

Registration of Marriage under Mediaeval Roman Law (Montmorency), 14 Society of Comparative Legislation (London, 1914).

Marriage by Reputation, 45 Law Journal (London, 1910).

Development of Marriage Law, 44 Law Journal (London, 1909).

Marriage and Divorce in Old Rome, Rogers, 18 Green Bag 402, (1906).

Common Law Marriage, R. C. Brickell, 44 American Law Review (1910).

Evidence of Common Law Marriage, 39 Central Law Journal 224 and 45 Central Law Journal 430.

Marriage Law in Savagery, J. W. Powell, 4 Science Monthly, 471 (New York).

Marriage by Mail, 32 Harvard Law Review 848-853 (1919).

Requisites and Proof of Common Law Marriage, 27 Harvard Law Review, 378-380 (1914).

Marriage by Mail, R. Gallagher, 5 Lawyer and Banker, 516 (1919).

Marriage by Letter, 22 Law Notes, (1919).

Act Relating to Uniform Marriage Law, 18 Law Notes, 128-132 (1914).

Proof of Common Law Marriage, 13 Law Notes 26 (1909).

Cohabitation as Essential to Common Law Marriage, 3 Minnesota Law Review 426-428 (1919).

Validity of Common Law Marriage as Affected by Statute, 12 Virginia Law Register 1.

Marriage at Common Law, 101 Law Times, (London) 575.

Marriage by Habit and Repute in England, 71 Law Times (London) 352.

Good Faith as a Test of Common Law Marriage, 9 Michigan Law Review 54.

Removal of Impediment of Common Law Marriage, 6 Michigan Law Review 247.

Marriage by Proxy, 8 Legal Adviser 47 (Chicago).

Cohabitation as Evidence of Marriage, 16 Irish Law Times 450.

Distinction between English and Scotch Law of Marriage, Redfield, 3 American Law Register (N. S.) 193.

Marriage by Repute, 3 Chicago Legal News, 227.

Common Law Marriage, Note to People vs. Shaw, 9 Illinois Law Review 214-218.

Cohabitation as Marriage where it begins unlawfully, 14 Lawyers Reports Annotated 364.

Common Law Marriage in New York, Effect of Statutes, 1 Cornell Law Quarterly 48-53.

Cohabitation as Essential to Common Law Marriage, 64 University of Pennsylvania Law Review, 406.

Evidence and Proof of Common Law Marriage in Civil and Criminal Cases (Texas) 14 Michigan Law Review, 499.

12

Requisites of Common Law Marriage, Marriage by Telephone, 21 Law Notes 142.

Removal of Impediment of Common Law Marriage, 27 Yale Law Journal 702 and 28 Yale Law Journal 515.

Common Law Marriage (Ill.) 13 Illinois Law Review, 540.

Gospel of Marriage According to Bishop, 13 Illinois Law Review, 34.

Marriage by Telephone, 24 Case and Comment 907.

Schaff Herzog, Encyclopedia of Religious Literature, Subjects, Marriage, Council of Trent, Sacraments.

The Geography of Marriage or Legal Perplexities of Marriage in The United States, Wm. L. Snyder, New York, 1889.

Contracts, Parsons, 8th Edition, Vol. II.

American Marriage Laws, Russell Sage Foundation 1919 (Hall and Brooke).

English Domestic Relations 1487-1653, Chilton Latham Powell, Columbia University Press, 1917.

This list does not include the many decisions of the courts consulted nor the many statutes of the Colonial period. They have been referred to in the text where they are of importance.

INDEX

	PAGE
Alabama, Early Decision in Support of Doctrine	96
American Colonies, Informal Marriages in	54
Beamish v. Beamish (English case following precedent admitted to be incorrect)	47
California, Early Decision in Support of Doctrine	94
Campbell, Lord, Decision of, in Millis Case	41
His Reference to America	44
Opposition of, to the Common Law Marriage	90
Cheseldine v. Brewer (Md.), (1739)	76
Children of Informal Marriages Could Not Inherit	19
Of Informal Marriages Legitimate	19
Cohabitation, Necessity of	116–138
Colonial Marriage Laws	54
Common Law Marriage, After the Removal of Impediment	153
Definition of	7
Held by Sup. Ct. of Dela. to be Contrary to American Institutions	69
Not Fully Recognied Anywhere	148
Opposed by American Bar Association	167
Opposed by Lord Campbell	90
Opposed by Commissioners on Uniform State Laws	167
Popular Notion of	102–103
Common Law Wife, New York Court's Definition of the Term	104
Connecticut Colony, Marriage in	60
Consummation, Necessity of, by Early Canon Law	14
Council of Trent	22
Canons and Decrees of, Touching Matrimony	24
Marriage Prior to	11
Dalrymple Case	37
De Anesty, Richard, Case of	20
Decretal of Alexander III	20
Decretum Reformatione Matrimonii, Council of Trent	22
Definition, Common Law Marriage	7
Delaware, Colonial Marriage Laws	65
Del Heith's Case	50
Doubt, Parties May Doubt Validity of Their Informal Marriage	107
Dower, Widow of Informal Marriage did not Take	18
English Marriage Act of 1753	29–32
Fenton v. Reed (New York) Kent's Decision	79
Fleet Marriages	30
Foxcroft's Case	50

PAGE

Georgia, Early Decision in Support of Doctrine 95
    Colonial Marriage Laws 65
Great Northern Railway v. Johnson (Fed.) 124
Hardwicke's (Lord) Act 29–32
Illinois, Early Decision in Support of Doctrine 96
Impediment, Removal of 153
Iowa, Decision in Support of Doctrine 97
Jewell v. Jewell (U. S.) Supreme Court Divided 91
Kent, Chancellor, Early Dictum in Support of Common Law Mar-
    riage 79
    His Commentaries 88
Kentucky, Early Decision in Support of Doctrine 86
Lateran Council 12
Legitimacy of Children of Informal Marriages at Common Law .. 50–53
Lombardian Classification 15
Luther, Martin, Protest Against Lombardian Distinctions 17
Madon, Martin, Criticism of English Marriage Act 35
Mail, Marriage by 133
Mangue v. Mangue (Mass.) 77
Marriage Act, English Act of 1753 29–32
    Harshness of 35
Marriage, Jurisdiction Over, at Common Law 13
Marriage, Proof of, from Cohabitation and Repute 148
Maryland, Colonial Marriage Laws 62
    Early Informal Marriage Case in 76
Massachusetts, Earliest Case of Informal Marriage 77
    Early Case Rejecting Common Law Rule 81
    Marriage in New Plymouth 58
Meister v. Moore (U. S.) Supreme Court Accepts Doctrine 99
Michigan, Decision in Support of Doctrine 97
Milford v. Worcester (Mass.) Doctrine Rejected 81
Millis Case, Regina v. Millis, English Case in 1843 Rejected the
    Doctrine 39
Minnesota, Decision in Support of Doctrine 98
Mississippi, Early Decision in Support of Doctrine 94
Missouri, Decision in Support of Doctrine 97
Nebraska, Secret Marriages Disapproved in 113
New Hampshire, Early Decision in Support of Doctrine 84
    Later Decision Against Doctrine 85
New Jersey, Colonial Marriage Laws 67
    Early Decision in Support of Doctrine 89
New York, Marriages in New Netherlands 67
North Carolina, Colonial Marriage Laws 66
Ohio, Early Decision in Support of Doctrine 96
Pennsylvania, Colonial Marriage Laws 69
    Dicta in Early Case Upholding Doctrine 83

PAGE

Per Verba De Futuro Cum Copula, in the United States 138
In the Early Canon Law 143–144–145
Origin of 15
Per Verba De Præsenti, Origin of 15
Presence, Parties Need Not Be in Each Other's Presence 133
Priest, Presence of, Necessary After Council of Trent 23
Regina v. Millis 39
As Authority in England 46
Rhode Island, Colonial Marriage Laws 66
Rowland v. United States (Fed.) 159
Secret Marriages 108
Semper Præsumitur Pro Matrimonio 151
Shaw, Chief Justice (Mass.), Decision of, Against Common Law
Rule 81
South Carolina, Colonial Marriage Laws 67
States, Law by 161–166
Status Personarum, Must Be Intent to Change 105–108
Stowell, Lord, Opinion in Dalrymple Case 38
Opposition of, to the Common Law Marriage 90
Supreme Court of United States Affirms the Doctrine 99
Divided on Common Law Marriage in 1843 91
Errors of 99–103–111
Travers v. Reinhart (U. S.) 156
War, Marriage During the World War 133
Wilmington Trust Co. v. Hendrixson (Del.) 69
Vermont, Early Decision in Support of Doctrine 88
Later Decision Against 89
Virginia, Colonial Marriage Laws 64

ImTheStory.com